Social Investment and Institutional Change

This book focuses on the main institutional changes affecting the Social Investment approach as the framework for the European social agenda.

The contributions gathered address these issues from different angles, placing two fundamental issues at the centre of the analysis. The first concerns the promotion of the strategic actions of European institutions and the national governments aimed at making social investment a recovery priority in the Eurozone. The second aims to make the social investment approach compatible not only with a high road to growth, as it is in the Stock-Flow-Buffer scheme, but also with the right to balance market and non-market activities as a universal right linked to a different combination of working and living time.

It will be of interest to all scholars and students of social policy and European politics.

Andrea Ciarini is Associate Professor of Economic Sociology in the Department of Social and Economic Sciences, Sapienza University of Rome, Italy. His research interests concern social policies and welfare systems from a comparative European perspective.

Social Welfare Around the World
Series editor
Bent Greve
Roskilde University, Denmark

This series publishes high quality research monographs and edited books focusing on development, change in provision and/or delivery of welfare – with a primary focus on developed welfare states. The books provide overviews of themes such as pensions, social services, unemployment or housing, as well as in-depth analysis of change and impact on a micro level. The impact and influence of supranational institutions on welfare state developments are studied as are the methodologies used to analyse the ongoing transformations of welfare states.

www.routledge.com/Social-Welfare-Around-the-World/book-series/ASHSER1427

Social Investment and Institutional Change

Edited by Andrea Ciarini

Routledge
Taylor & Francis Group

LONDON AND NEW YORK

First published 2023
by Routledge
4 Park Square, Milton Park, Abingdon, Oxon OX14 4RN

and by Routledge
605 Third Avenue, New York, NY 10158

Routledge is an imprint of the Taylor & Francis Group, an informa business

British Library Cataloguing-in-Publication Data
A catalogue record for this book is available from the British Library

Library of Congress Cataloging-in-Publication Data
Names: Ciarini, Andrea, editor.
Title: Social investment and institutional change / edited by
    Andrea Ciarini.
Description: Abingdon, Oxon ; New York, NY : Routledge, 2023. |
    Series: Social welfare around the world | Includes bibliographical
    references and index.
Identifiers: LCCN 2022061821 (print) | LCCN 2022061822 (ebook) |
    ISBN 9781032439761 (hbk) | ISBN 9781032439778 (pbk) |
    ISBN 9781003369707 (ebk)
Subjects: LCSH: Public welfare—Europe. | Welfare state—Europe. |
    Europe—Social conditions.
Classification: LCC HV40 .S6165 2023 (print) | LCC HV40 (ebook) |
    DDC 361.3094—dc23/eng/20230407
LC record available at https://lccn.loc.gov/2022061821
LC ebook record available at https://lccn.loc.gov/2022061822

ISBN: 978-1-032-43976-1 (hbk)
ISBN: 978-1-032-43977-8 (pbk)
ISBN: 978-1-003-36970-7 (ebk)

DOI: 10.4324/9781003369707

Typeset in Baskerville
by Apex CoVantage, LLC

Contents

Figures

Tables

Contributors

Colin Crouch is Professor Emeritus at the University of Warwick, United Kingdom, and an external scientific member of the Max Planck Institute for the Study of Societies in Cologne, Germany. He was formerly a lecturer at the London School of Economics, the University of Oxford, and the European University Institute.

Silvia Girardi is a researcher at the Luxembourg Institute for Socio-Economic Research (LISER) and a PhD candidate at the Centre for Sociological Research of the KU Leuven (Belgium). She holds an MSc in Sociology and Social Research from the University of Trento, Italy, and an Advanced Master in Social Policy Analysis from KU Leuven.

Anton Hemerijck is Professor of Political Science and Sociology at the European University Institute in Fiesole. Between 2009 and 2013, he was Dean of the Faculty of Social Sciences at the Vrije Universiteit in Amsterdam. From 2013 to 2017, he was Centennial Professor of Social Policy at the London School of Economics and Political Science (LSE). His most recent publications include *Changing Welfare States* (Oxford 2013) and *The Uses of Social Investment* (Oxford 2017).

Massimo Paci is Professor Emeritus of Economic Sociology in the Department of Social and Economic Sciences, Sapienza University of Rome.

Valeria Pulignano is Professor of Sociology at the Centre for Sociological Research (CESO) of KU Leuven University (Belgium). She is currently Principal Investigator of the ERC Advanced Grant project: Resolving Precariousness: Advancing the Theory and Measurement of Precariousness Across the Paid/Unpaid Continuum. His research interests include the sociology of work, industrial (and labour) relations, and precarious work.

Stefano Ronchi is a research fellow at the University of Milan, where he works on comparative analysis of European welfare systems. He has been Max Weber Fellow at the European University Institute (Fiesole), Jos Berghman Visiting Scholar at KU Leuven, and InGrid Visiting Fellow at the Centre for Social Policy in Antwerp.

Presentation

Faced with economic stagnation, low-quality employment and – at the time of writing – the onset of a new deep recession caused by pandemic and the international crisis, European welfare states are subjected to unprecedented levels of pressure. Years of cuts, privatisations, and austerity, especially in those countries with the highest public debt, have weakened the public institutions, caught between the increasingly pressing demands for fiscal consolidation and the explosion of new needs that are not met by current social policies. When not subjected to linear cuts, social spending has still been conceived as a cost to be made compatible with the stagnant rates of the economy and certainly not as a long-term investment that could also support social and economic development. In a striking contradiction between the objectives set by the European social agenda and the budgetary constraints imposed by the European institutions themselves, the two dimensions of Europe – the social and the economic – have come into sharp contrast in the last decade.

The new crisis, which started with the pandemic, has further weakened the macro-economic picture, with consequent dramatic recessive effects. In terms of employment, the extension of social safety nets and various measures to support employment (reduction in working hours, subsidies, and various forms of facilitation for businesses) have partly offset the danger of a sudden explosion of unemployment. However, the recessionary effects have not been totally absent on the labour market, given the sharp decrease in working hours for the employed and a rise in the number of the inactive. Compared to the previous crisis – in particular the phase that began with the sovereign debt crisis in 2010 – when the ambitious objectives of the European social agenda were subordinated to fiscal containment and austerity policies, the quick response of the EU institutions has revealed a glimpse of a paradigm shift, with the suspension of the stability pact and the many constraints that had previously limited the fiscal space of member states, but above all with the launch of new European programmes, from *Sure* to the *Recovery Plan* for the relaunch of growth and social cohesion. Indeed, the fiscal rules of the European treaties remain suspended, not abolished. However, the Next Generation EU opens the way to a season of relaunching investments for growth and modernisation of welfare systems that stands in marked contrast to the previous phase. The expectations for a change of direction in Europe are justified by the peculiar traits of the current crisis and the more solidaristic approaches adopted to face the Covid crisis and relaunch public investments as an instrument of growth. However, the problems that affect the European social protection systems do not concern merely the social and economic effects of the health crisis. The complexity of these issues, from growing inequalities to in-work poverty to the consequences of the demographic and technological transition, is due to a number of processes. Some of these are related to structural and institutional factors, others to reforms and policy options that have had negative consequences for social protection.

The contributions gathered here address these issues from different angles, placing two fundamental issues at the centre of the analysis. The first concerns the promotion of the strategic action of the European institutions and the national governments aimed at making social investment a recovery priority in the Eurozone. The second aims to make the social investment approach compatible with non-market activities (care, civic, and voluntary commitments) as universal rights of citizens linked to a different combination of working time and living time. The thread that unites them can be summarised as follows: the relaunching of a social investment agenda is part of an alternative social model to that of austerity, which has dominated in recent years. Nevertheless, not everything can be traced back to the importance, albeit strategic, *Stock*, *Flow* and *Buffer*, that is long-term investments in human capital *Stock* to raise labour productivity and skill to be spent in the labour market, in work-life *Flows* and inclusive *Buffers* to cushion the economic and social shocks. The search for solutions that aim to strengthen investments in these welfare policy fields does not preclude issues that also regard the balancing of market and non-market spheres of activity in relation to the profound social, economic, and technological changes we are currently experiencing.

The analysis proposed here refers to an institutional, national, and European framework, that is not unrealistic; indeed in some cases, it is already beginning to emerge, albeit in its early stages and not without contradictions, a sign that the outcomes are still open. The changes that are taking place in the economic and social structures require a general rethinking of the instruments of social protection, their aims, and the needs they are called to respond to. This rethinking leads us to ask questions about instruments that are perhaps still on the horizon but that in the future will be necessary to couple growth and social cohesion differently compared to the recent past.

1 Introduction

Investments and social policies in the years of the crisis

Andrea Ciarini

1.1 Supply and demand for social protection in the Great Recession

In the midst of the health crisis, recession, and new demands for social protection, the European welfare states today find themselves under the pressure of an almost unprecedented and urgent need for reorganisation. Years of cuts, privatisations, and austerity, especially in those countries with the highest public debt, have weakened the public institutions, caught between the increasingly pressing demands for fiscal consolidation and the explosion of new needs that are not met by current social policies. The new crisis, which started with the pandemic, has further weakened the macroeconomic picture, with consequent dramatic recessive effects. With the pandemic, European governments were faced with an unprecedented health and economic emergency. For the first time after years of cuts and ideological attacks on the state, the importance of the welfare state, public health, and redistributive interventions returned to the centre of public discourse. From this point of view, if the outbreak of the health crisis made clear the market's inability to meet the demand for social protection, the institutions were charged with responsibilities that would have been unthinkable until recently. From the launch of the SURE programme to the Next Generation EU, the European institutions and member states have brought about an unprecedented change in European macroeconomic governance by drawing on a common budget. In the previous phase, structural reforms denied any room for national institutions, especially with regard to the most indebted countries, imposing cuts in public spending, privatisations, and ultimately a subordination of social protection arrangements to purely financial logics. Several scholars have underlined the open contradiction between the ambitious objectives of the European social agenda and the strenuous defence, by the European institutions themselves, of austerity and fiscal containment policies, especially towards those countries that have been most affected by the crisis and therefore most in

DOI: 10.4324/9781003369707-1

need of the fiscal space to absorb the social costs (see also Hemerijck and Ronchi in this volume).

With the health emergency, the Stability Pact was suspended and states were able to deploy resources that had an effect on social emergencies and stabilisation of the economic cycle. And yet, the problems that today weigh on social protection systems do not only concern the effects of the crisis or the impact of the monetary union with its growing internal asymmetries. The complexity of such issues – from growing inequalities, to poverty, to low-quality employment despite the economic recovery – depends on a plurality of processes, some relating to structural and institutional factors, others to very specific policy choices by national governments which over the years have contributed to worsening rather than improving the effectiveness of welfare policies. Think of the widespread 'tolerance' towards inequalities typical of neoliberalism (Atkinson 2015; Stiglitz 2019; Piketty 2017) and the *trickle-down economics* of the 1980s, according to which tax cuts for the benefit of the wealthy actually favour the whole of society, including the lower-middle classes and those at the margins, because in this way investments and consumption by the rich are more likely, thus creating jobs even for the poorest. The implication has, for a long time, been the acceptance of social inequality and cuts in social spending, public services, and the reach of the state, seen as an element that disturbs market equilibrium, dissipating public resources and creating distortions in the allocation of social spending. Though the impact of neoliberal ideology cannot be overlooked and inequalities and precarious work are not the natural destiny of the economy, nevertheless there are also other factors of a structural and institutional nature that have contributed to determining certain outcomes and influencing policy choices.

Let us look at these factors in more detail. The first, of a structural nature, concerns the transition to the so-called 'knowledge society', a transition that is neither painless nor immune from new dualisms (Emmeneger et al. 2012). The outsourcing of the economy, the decline of employment in manufacturing, and the rise of new jobs requiring a high knowledge content have been interpreted in the past as a process of gradual qualitative enrichment of work and professionalism on a large scale. In reality, alongside the skilled labour of high productivity services and high wages (which is growing), the spectrum of 'poor' tertiary jobs, with low productivity and low wages, characterised by precariousness, has also widened, with a direct effect on the growth of inequalities and the widening of the gaps in the levels of social protection. This transformation, a parallel process of *upgrading* for some (those who manage to take advantage of the leap towards the knowledge society) and *downgrading* for others (those who suffer these transformations and are pushed to the margins of the labour market), is an integral part of the transition towards a service economy. The increase in employment in the tertiary sectors is much more exposed than in the past to the problem of working poverty and low wages, despite having contributed to increasing the overall employment rates in the labour market. The result is an employment structure in which inequalities are growing (in terms of wages and also in terms of social protection) between 'core' groups with high productivity of high value-added services and groups at the periphery, employed in less skilled tertiary jobs, often alternating between low-wage jobs and working poverty (Emmeneger et al. 2012).

Welfare services and social work in general are one of the areas in which this *trade-off* between employment and low-wage work is most visible. Within these sectors, employment has grown a lot in recent years and will continue to grow even more in the future due to the impact of demographic changes – think of the impact of the ageing population. The problem is that this expansion is determined by low wages, without a fair balance in terms of quality of work and remuneration (Colombo et al. 2011; Favarque 2013; Ciarini 2016). Here emerges one of the crucial points of the ongoing transition. These services (like all labour-intensive tertiary sectors) structurally coexist with low labour productivity, as a consequence of their relational nature, that is, the necessary co-presence of 'producer' and 'consumer' at the time of the provision of the service (see Eichhorst and Marx 2012). This characteristic, which refers to the well-known Baumol cost disease (Esping-Andersen 2002), contributes to the fact that wages are on average lower than in other sectors (industrial above all, but also the advanced tertiary sector), in which the presence of *capital-intensive* technologies supports productivity growth and consequently also wages. As has been highlighted in a wide range of literature (Iversen and Wren 1998; Esping-Andersen 2000; Carbonnier and Morel 2015), the problem of cost disease can only be solved in one of the following ways: either with the provision of public services (and therefore public employment) or through levels of social spending such as to bridge the differences in productivity that private, market, and third sector solutions offload on labour costs, fuelling the growth of low-wage work.

But how can we develop employment in the field of providing services to people, be it related to the care of the elderly, childcare, healthcare, or work-life balance, given their structural low unit productivity or the increasing costs that these services require? Not being able to count on high public spending to cover the productivity gap, the implication is a large share of low-skilled and low-paid work that grows in private market services. On the other hand, this is also the result of explicit policy choices, with reforms that have deliberately aimed at favouring low-cost work or the privatisation of services (Emmenger et al. 2012).

Another process that is contributing to the profound modification of the rifts that run through the social protection systems is the so-called polarisation. In general terms, it refers to the combined provision of an increase in more highly skilled as well as less skilled employment on the one hand, and a decrease in averagely skilled employment on the other (Goos and Manning 2007; Autor 2015; Bachmann et al. 2019). The resulting displacement effect contributes to making the labour market even more complex. In fact, alongside the dualism between *high skilled* and *low skilled* (Palier and Thelen 2010), the polarisation process also adds the problem of the downwards slide of the medium skilled (and medium protected up to now) workers, with the immediate effect of increasingly stronger competition to carry out those low-skilled jobs (Marchal and Marx 2018) and therefore a further downward spiral in the spread of working poverty.

The factors behind this situation are many. For many scholars (Autor 2015; Eichhorst et al. 2016), the main reason concerns the routinisation of work duties due to the technologies applied to work, with the effect of a downward displacement that crushes medium-skilled workers. As has been pointed out in these studies, technological change does not impact work in general, rather it tends to differentiate according to the degree of replicability and standardisation of the various work tasks, regardless of their intellectual or manual nature. To date, we are unable to say whether and to what extent technology will contribute to creating more jobs in the future than it replaces. The impacts estimated remain mixed between those who see the danger of a new mass technological unemployment in the process of digitisation (Brynjolfsson and McAfee 2014; Frey and Osborne 2017) and those who instead lean towards more prudent interpretations, also focusing on the compensatory effects (Autor 2015). What the empirical evidence does tell us at this stage is that we are facing a progressive shrinkage of the medium-skilled groups, which contributes to swelling the ranks of low-skilled and low-paid work that is already growing in the low-productivity tertiary sector (see Chapter 6 by Ciarini).

At the beginning of the 2000s, the concept of social vulnerability (Rosanvallon 1995; Castel 1995) was introduced in the literature to account for the entry into a new phase, different from the Fordist one, in which the main problem no longer consisted in the protection of 'wage' labour (Castel 1995) or in the exclusion of large sections of the population by the mechanisms of income redistribution, rather in the coexistence of different forms of fragility, at family, work, economic, and housing levels, which began to destabilise the life courses of increasingly heterogeneous groups of people. Given its multidimensional character, social vulnerability presented itself as a condition distinct from poverty in the strictest sense, not definable on the basis of a simple economic or income parameter. It reflected the transition to a condition of general insecurity that cut across the whole of society and a higher and more heterogeneous number of people, neither poor nor marginalised, yet in some moments at risk of fragility due to the progressive weakening of the three main pillars upon which the scaffolding of Fordist welfare was built: the stable labour market, the nuclear family, and the welfare state based on the (ex-post) response to circumstantial and random needs, therefore with a low probability of lasting any length of time (Mingione 1997).

Compared to this recent past, the changes affecting the demand for social protection at different latitudes exacerbate the risks of chronicisation of needs, especially for what concerns one of the poles of vulnerability, namely labour, given the growing number of *working poor* and low-wage workers. The precarious nature of work and low-quality employment are certainly not new phenomena. Already before 2008 it had been highlighted by many that the trend in employment growth had been matched neither by a substantial improvement in working conditions nor, more importantly, by a reduction in relative poverty rates (Cantillon 2011). However, the financial crisis and the Great Recession have exacerbated these trends. According to Ferrera (2019), three elements contribute today to redefining the contours of precariousness as a 'structural' position in society, rather than episodic or contingent: unstable and discontinuous activities or working relationships, inadequate or absent public support, particularly in periods of unemployment and vulnerable economic and family conditions, also due to low wages. But who are the *working poor* and what differentiates them from low-paid workers?

On a strictly statistical level, the *working poor* are employed individuals – or at least who were employed in the year of reference – whose equivalent family income (according to the common definition) is less than 60% of the national median income – corresponding to the relative poverty threshold (Marx and Nolan 2014; Lohmann and Marx 2018; Barbieri et al. 2018). This definition, commonly adopted in literature, is important because it delineates a phenomenon that is not an exclusive function of an individual's income, but of the family structure they belong to and the position in the labour market of all its members (Marx and Nolan 2014; Lohmann and Marx 2018). Such a criterion, as highlighted by Barbieri et al. (2018), implies the fact that an individual can be classified as *working poor*, living in a household at risk of poverty, regardless of individual income. This type of poverty is different and much more ambivalent than the classic condition of incapacity, because it is associated with a job that can even be dignified, yet is still insufficient for the number of people who make up the family unit.

Conversely, low-paid jobs refer to the income status of the individual worker, which by convention is set below the threshold of two-thirds of the median hourly wage (ibid). Second, though low-wage work, while arousing concern, is often seen as an alternative for the integration of low-productivity workers into the labour market, especially in low growth or crisis conditions, in the case of the *working poor* we are dealing with a 'socially' unacceptable phenomenon and, from this point of view, the bearer of greater regulatory implications (ibid.). The problem is that in many cases the policies implemented have not protected the beneficiaries from a reproduction of this phenomenon, on the contrary, running the risk of legitimising it, as if it were impossible to curb, and upon which to intervene either with practically predetermined forms of income support for low incomes or with real activation in the labour market. But as Chiara Saraceno (2016) made clear, it is not enough to increase employment to automatically reduce poverty, if one does not take into account what kind of employment and jobs are being supported through social security or created through social policies.

Regarding this problem, several scholars have highlighted how, while on the one hand, the strengthening of these policies has led to an increase in beneficiaries (no longer merely the most marginal strata of the population as was the case in the past), on the other, it has been conditioned by the idea of employment, above all for the purpose of favouring rapid reintegration into work, even at the price of precarious or low-paid jobs, albeit socially supported by minimum income (Marchal and Marx 2018). There are problems surrounding this point that are worth drawing attention to. On the one hand, in fact, conditions, active policies, and various tax credits to increase the net return on labour can play a positive role in alleviating passive dependence on subsidies (especially for those most at risk), yet on the other hand, this is not enough to guarantee job placement or qualify the job that is created.

And here we return to the problem of the links between structural processes and policy choices, with both their expected and unexpected effects. In Section 1.2, we will examine the transformations that have involved the main recalibration paradigm on which a European convergence perspective has been woven during the past years, namely social investment, which has not been exempt from criticism regarding its ability to counterbalance the pressure towards the spread of working poverty.

1.2   The challenges for the welfare state: social investment and the new needs brought about (not only) by the crisis

The chapter by Colin Crouch, which opens this volume, focuses on the paradigm of social investment as the inspiring frame for the European social agenda. In a framework of already tight budgetary constraints and in parallel with the exit from the old Fordist welfare system, based on the centrality of social insurance and on the passive protection of (old) risks associated with employed work (illness, disability, unemployment, and old age), the novelty of social investment came from the importance afforded to investments in education, active policies, and care and conciliation services, in a preventive logic oriented towards future returns. In the words of Esping-Andersen, to whom we owe the development of this approach – since the publication in 2002 of the now famous book *Why We Need a New Welfare State*, co-edited with Duncan Gallie, Anton Hemerijck and John Myles – the transition to this new type of policy had to respond to a twofold objective: on the one hand to increase the number of people active on the labour market, so as to broaden the welfare tax base with which to guarantee the sustainability of social spending in the long term, and on the other hand to improve human capital and labour productivity with investments in education, from early childhood, as the starting point of a long-term investment strategy on all stages of the life cycle.

This 'preventive' and future-oriented strategy, aimed at facilitating the transition from the old passive policies to the new generation of activating policies, has also been studied by Crouch, who has examined in a comparative key the effects on the level of social benefits and indirect returns on the labour market in various European countries.

The productivity of social spending that is promoted in this paradigm is very different from the traditional Keynesian-Fordist public interventionism which saw in the expansion of social spending a means, both of protection from the risks associated with employee work, and of growth of domestic demand, albeit at the price of an excess of public debt. As Palier (2013) pointed out, compared to this phase (the glorious 1930s, which saw the incremental development of benefits), the purpose of social protection is no longer to contribute directly to full employment and to the redistribution of wealth with an eye to the stability of production and consumption. It is rather, indirectly, that social spending contributes to achieving these objectives, favouring active participation in the labour market, especially of those who are most at risk of being excluded – women due to family ties or lack of services, young people due to relative deficits in schooling and professional skills acquired – in an exchange between (decreasing) old passive policies and new activating policies designed to cope with the new risks linked to life cycles, not only with work.

It is a fact that this preventive and supply-side orientation (i.e. aimed at intervening on the components of the labour supply, without foreseeing anything in terms of aggregate demand policies) is very distant from Keynesianism. In the same way, however, it is also different from those approaches to reforms that are centred on the deregulation of the labour market and on the workfarist activation typical of the reductionist vision of neoliberalism, which sees dependence on passive subsidies as the main objective of the reforms. Compared to this generation of active policies, the social investment approach does not presuppose an overcoming of the supply-side approach. That is, the pre-eminence of the components of the job offer does not alter in the development of policies for job placement and reintegration. If anything, this centrality is recalibrated in a perspective of growth and strengthening of investments in education and learning throughout the course of life (life-long learning), as a strategic lever for development and job inclusion, especially for the new generations. There is also the recognition of the importance of the integrated welfare of social services, that is, of all those ranges of intervention that have allowed the Scandinavian countries to achieve advantageous positions (in terms of active participation in the labour market) compared to the countries of continental Europe and, even more so, than the Mediterranean countries, where welfare is still largely dominated by traditional insurance institutions and the policy of social services is practically absent.

Obviously, whether it is a matter of consolidating the results achieved or of bridging a gap, the prospect of social investment implies an additional investment in active policies for labour, training, care, and conciliation. On the other hand, the implication is the acceptance of a substantial downsizing of passive policies (pensions and passive labour policies) because they are no longer useful for providing effective responses to new needs and unsuitable for affecting the activation and employability of the beneficiaries.

Some scholars, such as Nolan (2013), have affirmed that the development of social investment is to be related to a general process of recommodification and *retrenchment* of the welfare state, due to the close relationship with the labour market as the main unit of measurement and evaluation of the social impacts of reforms. According to Crouch (see also Morel et al. 2012; Hemerijck 2013), we are faced with an attempt at synthesis to combine broad participation in the labour market with support for the growth and development of products with higher added value (see also Bonoli and Natali 2012). Of course, this combination is not automatic because, as Crouch reminds us in the same chapter, a social investment strategy is not in and of itself necessary in order to obtain a high level of employment, as shown, for example, by the United Kingdom, which couples high levels of employment with low social spending and *work-first* labour policies. Rather, a social investment strategy is crucial to supporting the transition to production specialisations with higher added value in international competition and to encouraging female participation in the labour market.

While over time these have become the pillars of social investment, rather than the discourse on the contrast of inequalities, some critical aspects have also come to the fore. Among them, we must mention the assumption that the financial markets will remain stable, which the 2008 crisis revealed to be inaccurate (see Crouch again in this volume), and secondly, an excessive stigmatisation of the 'old', 'passive' social protection policies which is a result of the implicit distinction made between social expenses worth investing on because they are 'productive' (active labour policies, training, care and conciliation) and expenses on which to accept cuts because they are unproductive (pensions and passive labour policies). Finally, the tendency of the most qualified workers – the *high-skilled workers* of the advanced tertiary sector – to take greater advantage of activating policies at the expense of the less qualified and the weakest beneficiaries – the so-called 'Matthew effect' (see Cantillon 2011; Cantillon and Van Lancker 2013; Bonoli et al. 2017) – from the passage of the Gospel according to Matthew, which says: *For whosoever hath, to him shall be given and he shall have more abundance; but whosoever hath not, from him shall be taken away even that he hath.*

Crouch concludes his reflection by reminding us that social investment is not the only way to support the labour market. However, it is a policy approach that is useful in avoiding the trap of competition based merely on prices – that is, on the low cost of labour – which brings with it production specialisations in low value-added activities. And yet, as Crouch points out, the high road to competitiveness, while on the one hand favours the qualification and productivity of labour, on the other it does not solve the problems of those exposed to job instability and insecurity. Faced with the risk of a growing divide between 'winners' and 'losers' of the 'post-industrial transition', what certainly emerges is the need to strengthen the forms of income protection for the new 'excluded', starting with those to support income, as was also recognised by Hemerijck (2017); see also Hemerijck and Ronchi in this volume) in his reformulation of the institutional foundations of social investment. These can be summarised in the triangulation between: (1) *Stock* – investments in training and human capital for the whole life span; (2) *Flow* – active labour policies and conciliation services between work and care tasks; (3) *Buffer* – inclusive income protection and social safety nets. Compared to the first thematisations on social investment, there is, in this new articulation of interventions, a recognition of the necessary integration between actions to support the transition towards higher value-added sectors and income protection measures in the form of guaranteed minimum income and social safety nets. This is one of the main challenges for European welfare states, together with the problem of scarce resources that do not allow for expansionary manoeuvres on social spending until recent years, especially for countries that have less fiscal space due to the constraints of austerity. So often there has been an attempt to reallocate items of expenditure between policy areas in search of a balance that is difficult to achieve but that risks having an impact on the widening of inequalities between those who manage to place themselves in the upper reaches of the labour market and those who, instead, find themselves trapped in working poverty.

In actual fact, the downward plots concern several policy areas and a wide variety of reforms that have tried either to preserve or to reach (depending on the case) some recalibration objectives (such as the strengthening of active labour policies, the growth of coverage rates of care services, and the strengthening of income support measures), but at the price of new and deeper trade-offs: *between growth in coverage rates for care services and low-wage employment in these same services; between job placement and employment at risk of working poverty, even when subsidised by minimum income schemes.*

The presence of these is common in many European countries, even in those less affected by the economic and financial crisis. Their intensity, links of reciprocal functionality and internal consistency within each national context are, however, different. Another element to highlight is that all this does not imply an automatic regression of the public sphere. What emerges is, rather, a type of public action aimed at supporting, explicitly or otherwise, the development of these new junctures. They make it possible to keep social spending under control and, in part, also reorient the welfare offer towards new social risks, producing, however, negative effects that are discharged either onto the beneficiaries of the services or onto the social workers. These problems are accounted for in Chapters 2 and 3, starting with a critical examination of the transformations that have characterised two central areas of social investment: poverty reduction and care services.

1.3 Poverty reduction and the workfarist shift of minimum income policies

The chapter by Ciarini, Girardi, and Pulignano focuses on minimum income policies. All European countries, and more recently even Italy, have adopted measures of this type, built on a mix, which varies from country to country, of transfers for income support and services for social and labour inclusion. In this sense, the guaranteed minimum income falls within the assistance measures for people who find themselves in a situation of serious economic hardship. From this point of view, these must be clearly distinguished from the basic income perspective, as a universal transfer for all citizens, unconditional and free from obligations of work placement (Van Parijs and Vanderborght 2019). Also, due to the crisis on minimum income, many expectations have poured out in recent years, not only the (original) one of coping with situations of extreme poverty but also that of income support for the working poor (Natili 2018). The problem, as shown in Chapter 2, is that the redistributive scope of these policies has been decreasing. This downward pressure is also due to the changes in the productive structure with the transition to the knowledge society and the new dualisms that ensued (see Emmenegger et al. 2012). In addition to these problems, the economic crisis has generated further impacts, which have led not only to an increase in unemployment but also to the use of flexible forms of employment, part-time contracts and low concentration of working hours, which have increased the amount of low working wages, especially in the lower tertiary sector (Marchal and Marx 2018). Then there is the issue of its distribution by family composition and by levels of education. Finally, gender and age also constitute variables. These different factors, which vary from country to country, have a direct impact on the spread of poverty, despite employment. The point we are interested in highlighting here is that this phenomenon is also a reflection of political choices that have changed the role of minimum income in the direction of a stronger link with the labour market, at the cost, however, of decreasing the intensity of redistributive effects and the ability to counter the risk of poverty.

As has already been said, compared to an initial phase in which the minimum income was essentially conceived as a welfare measure in favour of the poor, over the years it has undergone an activating twist, to the point of becoming, in many cases, also an instrument of income support for *working poor*, economically supported but still at the limit of, or below, the (relative) poverty line. This work-first twist in in the efforts to achieve poverty reduction naturally also calls into question active labour market policies, which in turn are subjected to a further conditioning twist. The 'activating torsion' was, after all, introduced to strengthen the incentive to work. It is no longer just a question of maintaining a financial incentive (ensuring a differential between the guaranteed minimum income and the minimum wage) but of forcing the beneficiaries to seek employment opportunities (subsidised, paid, and unpaid in community service activities) in exchange for welfare support.

One of the ambivalent aspects of this shift concerns the effects on work, not only that which exists and towards which the beneficiaries of the services are directed but also that which is created through the various tools designed to promote employment opportunities. It is from this perspective that the reform strategies pursued by some of the main European countries, Germany, Denmark, France, and Italy, will be examined. The questions to be answered here are the following: Through which mechanisms do the various measures for poverty reduction affect the reconfiguration of the relationship between paid work and income support? Which spheres of activation, paid and unpaid, does minimum income include? Finally, what implications do these active strategies have on the way of conceiving and regulating work?

1.4 Care services and social work: a wider reach at the price of low-paid work?

In an analysis of the problems that still insist on the European social agenda, other trade-offs can also be identified, in a line of continuity with those already outlined earlier. Changes in the institutional organisation of welfare supply affect not only the nature and scope of social provision but also the care labour market. We deal with this in Chapter 3. The adoption of a social investment strategy necessarily implies an expansion of social services and the employment that is generated within them. This is primarily due to the need to encourage a wider participation in the labour market, by strengthening work-life balance and the provision of personal and household services. Although differences in national settings remain, the potential of these services in terms of job creation has also been widely recognised by European institutions. The *Employment Package* and the *Social Investment Package*, launched by the European Commission in 2012 and 2013, granted special attention to the employment potential of these services. Nevertheless, they are facing several challenges. As much analysis has shown (European Commission 2012; Colombo et al. 2011; European Commission 2015), working conditions are characterised by a high incidence of low-paid and low-qualified jobs, high female segregation, and a strong variety of employment relations, including an expanding low-paid workforce at home. This is already an element of interest, but even more so is the fact that this work is an integral part of the expanding labour demand which will continue to expand in the future despite the crisis and regardless of the policy choices, because it is driven by structural factors, concerning the great demographic transformations and the internal changes to families.

As we will show in this part of the book, the employment data for these sectors clearly show a growth dynamic, though each country has its specific characteristics. There are in fact countries that have traditionally focused on the growth of public employment (traditionally the entire Scandinavian grouping) or private employment outside the family (the United Kingdom) and countries, such as Italy, in which formal employment is lower compared to the prevalence of informal work within families. Finally, there are countries in which the increase in social benefits has been driven by a mix of formal and informal employment, through vouchers and fiscal credits for families that have favoured job creation in the personal and household services sector.

The problem that many European countries are facing is that this growth in employment has rewarded (even before the crisis) an increase in the number of jobs, without equal development in terms of the qualification of the employment created, which often means low-paid jobs and an emerging juncture between poor jobs and minimum income schemes. By focusing on three European countries: Germany, France, and Italy, in this chapter we illustrate how the strategies to boost regular employment in the care services sector have had a pivotal link with the minimum income schemes, seen as measures that help to integrate and reproduce low paid jobs. A typical example of a model that fuels low-wage labour at risk of poverty, despite the existence of a minimum income, are the reforms introduced both in France and especially in Germany, where the expansion of service provision was driven by a wide expansion of low-wage work in personal and household services, albeit subsidised by minimum income schemes (see also Chapter 3 by Ciarini, Pulignano, and Girardi). In both cases, we are faced with a growing share of workers who are regularly employed, either in families or by private providers, yet still at risk of poverty, who receive the minimum income.

In the case of Italy, the issue is even more complicated, due to the fact that not only is it more heavily conditioned by the familistic orientation inherited from the past as well as by a low expenditure on care policies, but also because of the absence in recent years of a defined development strategy for personal and household services. It is rather the undeclared work that has driven this development, with repercussions that are even worse compared to other countries, due to the large basin of irregular work that persists in the care system, and the inadequacy, at least until recent years, of poverty reduction policies.

1.5 The relaunch of the European social agenda: transferring investments for human capital stocks and care and conciliation services out of the stability pact

Chapter 5 by Hemerijck and Ronchi continues the analysis of social investment policies. The objectives set by this paradigm remain of fundamental importance in order to improve human capital (*Stock*) and support a continuous qualification of work and of the sectors with the highest productivity. Equally important, however, is investing in *Flow* (active labour market policies and care and work-life balance) as well as in *Buffers*, that is, income support. The main problem, according to the two authors, is that many countries still lack a balanced portfolio regarding these three functions. In times of austerity, fiscal consolidation leaves little room for the expansion of investments in the core area of the social investment approach. In the last few years its repercussions disregarded any hypothesis of relaunching public investments, with negative effects on social cohesion, employment and also on labour productivity. According to the authors, policy response to the COVID-19 pandemic marked a turn towards the (re-)appreciation of public investment to relaunch growth and social cohesion. This opened a new window of opportunity for real social investment reform in member states adversely affected by the Great Recession and the pandemic. Against the backdrop of a devastating public health crisis with unprecedented diffuse social and economic consequences and experiential learning from the mistakes made during the Euro crisis, EU institutions have a concrete opportunity to relaunch a far more solidaristic approach to social cohesion. This means a more assertive EU-level social investment agenda in terms of poverty mitigation through inclusive minimum income protection *Buffers*, which remain a prerequisite for an effective social investment strategy, and investments in human capital *Stocks* and labour market and life-course *Flows*. Against this background, Hemerijck and Ronchi focus on some of the emerging tools to mitigate unemployment risks and boost inclusive growth at a European level: the (temporary) SURE plan and the RRF, the key instrument at the heart of the Next Generation EU to raise funds to help member states implement reforms and investments in line with the EU's priorities with a total budget of €723.8 billion (385.8 in loans and 338 in grants). While SURE provides support to short-time work schemes (to retain jobs and prevent unemployment), the RRF creates a fiscal space to enhance the Union's economic, social, and territorial cohesion and convergence beyond the mitigation of the socio-economic consequences of the COVID-19 crisis and the further integration of the EU economies.

According to Hemerijck and Ronchi, the RRF is far more promising compared to the SURE, which implies practical and institutional problems. First, any effective EU social insurance mechanism depends on the variegated design of national unemployment systems in terms of coverage, activation, and income protection. Second, even when balancing national and European levels, the fact remains that social insurances typically protect insiders rather than outsiders. As pointed out by the authors, effective and more inclusive minimum income Buffers are crucial to provide income support to those who are outside of the coverage of social insurance and have been strongly affected by the social and economic consequences of the pandemic. In this respect, the RRF is far more promising as it creates a genuine fiscal space that links investments to socio-economic reforms aimed at fostering a viable division of responsibilities between the EU and the member states to support the three policy functions of social investment. Especially for countries struggling to commit to a balanced budget without abandoning their buffering social protection commitments, the RRF could foster immediate gains in early childhood, female employment, improved work-life balance, and reduced levels of early school leaving, with positive medium-term outcomes in employment growth, productivity through higher educational attainment, and ultimately a lower pension burden resulting from higher levels of employment. Hemerijck and Ronchi conclude their analysis with a more assertive relaunch of the social investment agenda. As the RRF is about capital expenditures, not current expenditures, there is the risk to increase investments in social infrastructure at the expense of labour costs, which could remain devaluated. This brings back the risk of a low-road to social investment, negatively affected by the raise of low-paid jobs at the margins of the labour market, as it was during the last decades in many European countries. As pointed out by the authors, a more assertive EU-level social investment strategy requires a fiscal approach that privileges both current and capital expenditures. This means that we need economic policies that incorporate social goals and social policies aimed at promoting decent jobs, not only in the core sector of the labour market but also at the periphery of the service economy, where wages and working conditions are worse and the risk of poverty more widespread.

1.6 Social investment and the pluri-active society

The changes taking place in the EU macro-economic governance reflect an attempt to make social investment a recovery priority in the Eurozone. This means making all European countries able to both absorb the economic and social aftershocks and promote a 'productive' shift of the social expenditure. Nevertheless, looking at the future of the European social model, not everything can be traced back to the strategic importance of the three policy functions of social investment. As pointed out in the chapter by Hemerijck and Ronchi, the relaunching of investments in the SI is part of an alternative social model to that of austerity, which has dominated in recent years. Nevertheless, not everything can be traced back to the importance, albeit strategic, of *Stock*, *Flow*, and *Buffer*. The search for solutions aimed at supporting the creation of jobs in highly skilled, high-value-added sectors does not preclude issues that also regard the balancing of market and non-market spheres of activity in which people participate to the society. In the SI framework, the way the balancing between Stock, Flow and Buffer is promoted is essentially instrumental to productive goals. Encouraging women's employment, as well as supporting work-life balance and family policies, is more functional to raise labour productivity and active labour market participation, rather than allowing women to develop their capabilities in both market- and non-market-oriented activities, such as caregiving and volunteering, (Saraceno C. 2017). Additionally, the work-first twist that affected minimum income schemes in many European countries (see Ciarini, Girardi, and Pulignano in this volume) included non-market community service activities as a condition for accessing the benefit. This means making non-market and unpaid activities instrumental to getting a paid job, rather than promoting human capabilities within and outside the labour market. In the final chapter, Ciarini and Paci focus on these different productive and reproductive links, in light of the profound changes that are affecting income support policies as a consequence of the digital transition. As already stated, the displacement effects on medium-skilled jobs currently resulting from technological change and digitisation further exacerbate the issues of income protection. Under the impulse of technological change, labour markets are in fact undergoing a qualitative change that fuels the increase of highly skilled and high-value-added jobs. But overall, it is plausible that this process has involved a relatively few number of workers. At the same time, the parallel reduction of medium-skilled jobs tends to increase the incidence of low-skilled and low-paid work. This change is structural and far beyond the effects of the current economic crisis, putting under pressure not only middle class but also income support policies, as they evolved until the last years. Faced with the raise of beneficiaries and the pressure to reduce public spending, many countries reinforced working conditionalities, with a marked pressure to favour work at any cost, his often led to a system based on subsidies against poverty that legitimise and reproduce in-work poverty, in both paid and non-market unpaid community activities. The question at this point is the following: Is it possible to trace a possible alternative to this option? And to what extent can the structural transformations affecting work (outsourcing, polarisation, and digitalisation of the economy) be rebalanced by a different way of conceiving income support?

Based on the reflection presented in Chapter 6, various reform hypotheses are grouped into three main options. The first aims at strengthening social safety nets and poverty reduction policies so as to meet the requests for protection of those who are most at risk in the ongoing transition. Reforms that aim at strengthening unemployment benefits and minimum incomes can be included in this option. The second option concerns the establishment of an unconditional *basic income* for all, as a universal measure that concerns all citizens without any condition upon activation (Van Parijs and Vanderborght 2019). In this case, the *basic income* is configured as a universal income detached from the wage mechanism and as an alternative to work. Crouch has written in the first chapter of this volume that, even in the future, the work-welfare link will remain essential, far from the idea of a society without work to be compensated or indemnified with a citizenship income. Indeed, if it is clear that social spending can be hinged on a path of sustainability in the long term, first of all through an extension of the employment base, it is equally true that the wider the participation in the labour market, the more work is created, also through investments in welfare and above all in services. This naturally prompts us to look favourably on those social policies that focus on this objective. But at the same time, also on those aimed at freeing up time to devote to other activities, not mediated by a contract (therefore outside the formal conception of work), yet still having an economic and social value.

The third option that fits into this framework – unlike the other two – aims at a controlled reduction in market working hours and consequently at freeing up time in other spheres of economically and legally recognised non-market activity. This perspective does not suggest a differentiated strategy between the (few) winners and the losers of the technological transition, mirroring the double movement of polarisation and *upgrading*. Nor is it an alternative to market work, as is the case for many interpretations of the proponents of *basic income*, in view of a 'jobless' society to be compensated or indemnified with a universal dividend (Van Parijs and Vanderborght 2019). If anything, it envisages a reorganisation of the protection (for all) within a framework of controlled reduction of market working time towards a pluri-active society (Paci 2005) characterised by a high level of innovation and productivity, in which a series of socially recognised non-market activities (care, volunteering, education and training) are valued too, and are carried out by citizens on the basis of their preferences.

This option does not question the right to social assistance, nor does it look at a simple transition from old passive policies to new active ones. Rather, it moves within a perspective of a general rethinking of social protection in contexts in which different spheres of non-market activity acquire weight and social recognition along with paid work. In this interpretation of social investment there is a clear influence of the thinking of Sen (2000), in particular of the idea of a recognition of rights not only on the formal-normative level but on the substantive level, that is, relative to the concrete possibility of exerting one's rights, as the possibility of achieving the objectives that each believes are important for their own well-being, inside or outside the labour market. In these circumstances, substantive freedom to achieve certain states starting from individual preferences presupposes a type of public intervention that enables the subject to be able to make choices, not simply be compensated for damage suffered, and yet at the same time not to be forced to accept any job offer, or even unpaid work outside the labour market, as a condition to access some subsidy or guaranteed minimum income.

The debate on non-market activities is closely linked to the transformations we have just described. Between polarisation processes, poor jobs, and impacts of technology, it is likely that there will be consequences for the quantity and quality of work available. And some of them are already evident, as we have seen. In particular, the main problem today is the reduction of medium-skilled occupations, with the consequence of greater downward competition for the same jobs. The technology, however, does not prefigure only a displacement of work, but also a possible liberation of time given by the fact that more is produced with less job and in presence of gains of productivity or at least reduction of the costs for the enterprises. This aspect calls in cause different issues relative to the emergence of new social inequalities, for example, between those who suffer polarisation and those who instead manage to take advantage of the upgrading towards more qualified jobs. But no less important is to pose the problem of how to use gains in productivity to rebalance working time for all.

As in other phases of transition, the problem of rethinking the general structures of production and reproduction arises this time too. In the past, 'Work less, work for everyone' was a slogan used to redistribute market work. It may be that in the future it could be associated with specific safeguards aimed at enhancing the pluri-activity of individuals on an economic and legal level.

References

Atkinson, T. (2015) *Inequalities. What Can be Done.* Oxford: Oxford University Press.

Autor, D. (2015) Why are there still so many jobs? The history and future of workplace automation. *The Journal of Economic Perspectives*, 3, pp. 3–30.

Bachmann, R., Cim, M., Green, C. (2019) Long-run patterns of labour market polarization: Evidence from German micro data. *British Journal of Industrial Relations*, 57(2), pp. 350–376.

Barbieri, P., Cutuli, G., Scherer, S. (2018) In-work poverty in un mercato del lavoro duale: Individualizzazione riflessiva dei rischi sociali o stratificazione della diseguaglianza sociale? *Stato e Mercato*, 3, pp. 419–460.

Bonoli, G., Cantillon, B., Van Lancker, W. (2017) Social investment and the Matthew effect: Limits to a strategy. In: Hemerijck, A. (eds) *The Uses of Social Investment*. Oxford: Oxford University Press, pp. 66–76.

Bonoli, G., Natali, D. (2012) *The Politics of the New Welfare State*. Oxford: Oxford University Press.

Brynjolfsson, E., McAfee, A. (2014) *The Second Machine Age: Work, Progress, and Prosperity in a Time of Brilliant Technologies.* New York: W. W. Norton & Company.

Cantillon, B. (2011) The paradox of the social investment state: Growth, employment and poverty in the Lisbon era. *Journal of European Social Policy*, 21(5), pp. 432–449.

Cantillon, B., Van Lancker, W. (2013) Three shortcomings of the social investment perspective. *Social Policy and Society*, 12(4), pp. 553–564.

Carbonnier, C., Morel N. (eds.) (2015) *The Political Economy of Household Services in Europe.* Basingstoke: Palgrave Macmillan.

Castel, R. (1995) *Les Métamorphose de la question sociale. Unechronique du Salariat.* Paris: Fayard.

Ciarini, A. (2016) Policies to boost services and employment in the long-term care sector. A downward convergence towards low-wage service jobs in the European Welfare State? *Stato e Mercato,* 1, pp. 119–151.

Colombo, F., Nozal, A.L., Mercier, J., Tjadens, F. (2011) *Help Wanted? Providing and Paying for LTC.* Paris: OECD Health Policy Studies.

Eichhorst, W., Hinte, H., Rinne, U., Tobsch V. (2016) *How Big Is the Gig? Assessing the Preliminary Evidence on the Effects of Digitalization on the Labor Market.* IZA Policy Paper, n. 117, Bonn, October.

Eichhorst, W., Marx, P. (2012) Whatever works: Dualisation and the service economy in Bismarckian welfare states. In: Emmenegger, P., Häusermann, S., Palier, B., Seeleib-Kaiser, M. (eds.), *The Age of Dualization: The Changing Face of Inequality in Deindustrializing Societies.* Oxford: Oxford University Press, pp. 73–99.

Emmenegger, P., Häusermann, S., Palier, B., Seeleib-Kaise, M. (2012) *The Age of Dualization: The Changing Face of Inequality in Deindustrializing Societies.* Oxford: Oxford University Press.

Esping-Andersen, G. (2000) *I fondamenti sociali delle economie postindustriali.* Bologna: il Mulino.

Esping-Andersen, G., Hemerijck, A.E., Gallie, D.E., Myles, J. (eds) (2002) *Why We Need a New Welfare State.* Oxford: Oxford University Press.

European Commission. (2012) *Staff Working Document on Exploiting the Employment Potential of the Personal and Household Services.* Brussels: SWD.

European Commission. (2015) *Social Investment in Europe. A Study of National Policies 2015.* Brussels: Directorate-General for Employment, Social Affairs and Inclusion.

Favarque, N. (2013) *Developing Personal and Household Services in the EU. A Focus on Housework Activities* (Report for the DG Employment). Brussels: Social Affairs and Inclusion.

Ferrera, M. (2019) *La Società del Quinto Stato.* Bari-Roma: Laterza.

Frey, C.B., Osborne, M.A. (2017) The future of employment: How susceptible are jobs to computerisation? *Technological Forecasting and Social Change,* 114, pp. 254–280.

Goos, M., Manning, A. (2007) Lousy and lovely jobs: The rising polarization of work in Britain. *The Review of Economics and Statistics,* 89(1), pp. 118–33.

Hemerijck, A. (2013) *Changing Welfare States.* Oxford: Oxford University Press.

Hemerijck, A. (eds) (2017) *The Uses of Social Investment.* Oxford: Oxford University Press.

Iversen, T., Wren, A. (1998) Equality, employment, and budgetary restraint: The trilemma of the service economy. *World Politics,* 50(4), pp. 507–546.

Lohmann, H., Marx, I. (eds) (2018) *Handbook on In-Work Poverty.* Cheltenham: Edward Elgar Publishing.

Marchal, S., Marx, I. (2018) Stemming the tide: What have EU countries done to support low-wage workers in an era of downward wage pressures? *Journal of European Social Policy,* 28(1), pp. 18–33.

Marx, I., Nolan, B. (2014) In-work poverty. In: Cantillon, B., Vandenbroucke, F. (eds) *Reconciling Work and Poverty Reduction. How Successful Are European Welfare State?* Oxford, New York: Oxford University Press, pp. 131–156.

Mingione, E. (1997) *Sociologia della vita economica*. Roma: Carocci.

Morel, N., Palier, B., Palme, J. (2012) *Towards a Social Investment Welfare State? Ideas, Policies and Challenges*. Bristol: Policy Press.

Natili, M. (2018) The politics of minimum income. In: *Explaining Path Departure and Policy Reversal in the Age of Austerity*. London: Palgrave Macmillan.

Paci, M. (2005) *Nuovi Lavori, Nuovo Welfare*. Bologna: Il Mulino.

Palier, B., Thelen, K. (2010) Institutionalizing dualism: Complementarities and change in France and Germany. *Politics & Society*, 1, pp. 119–148.

Palier, B. (2013) Social policy paradigms, welfare state reforms and the crisis. *Stato e Mercato*, 1, pp. 37–66.

Piketty, T. (2017) *Capitale e disuguaglianza. Cronache dal mondo*. Milano: Bompiani.

Rosanvallon, P. (1995) *La nouvelle question sociale*. Seuil: Parigi.

Saraceno, C. (2017) Family relationships and gender equality in the social investment discourse: An overly reductive view? In: Hemerijck, A. (eds) *The Uses of Social Investment*. Oxford: Oxford University Press, pp. 59–65.

Stiglitz, J.E. (2019) *People, Power, and Profits: Progressive Capitalism for an Age of Discontent*. New York: W. W. Norton & Company.

Van Parijs P. Vanderborght Y. (2019) *Basic Income: A Radical Proposal for a Free Society and a Sane Economy*. Harvard: Harvard University Press.

2 The social investment welfare state

What can it achieve?

Colin Crouch

2.1 Introduction

The central contention of the strategy for a social investment welfare state (SIWS) is that social policy can be a major means for enabling work forces in the advanced economies to sustain their competitiveness in global markets – not by merely becoming cheaper, but by improving their skills and competences. This differs from prevailing views that social policy is at best a form of compensation for the losers of economic change and at worst a waste of money. Instead, it regards certain kinds of social policy as social infrastructure spending, analogous to spending on physical infrastructure – roads, railway systems, telecommunications networks, etc.

In its initial formulations in the 1990s, SIWS was rooted in the theory of new social risks (NSR), as developed by Anthony Giddens (1994, 1998) from the arguments of Ulrich Beck (1986) (see also Ferrera 1998; Taylor-Gooby 2004). Beck had originally argued that in the contemporary economy, the nature of risks facing working people had changed. In a past that he did not specify very clearly, ordinary people had experienced risk as a threat, and they needed protection from it; hence the original emphasis of 20th-century social policy on income maintenance in the face of risks of sickness, old age, unemployment, and disability. Today, he, and in particular Giddens, argued, these risks had been largely overcome, while contemporary workers in the new economy experienced new forms of risk as challenge and opportunity. If they were equipped with education and frequent opportunities for retraining, they could stay abreast of change, enabling the economies in which they worked to move into higher value-added activities, thereby avoiding being drawn into a downwardly spiralling competition with workers in the new low-wage economies of the far east and central and eastern Europe (CEE). Central to the new forms of employment were jobs in various service sectors, which employed women in far greater numbers than in the old manufacturing economy. Increased female employment, especially

DOI: 10.4324/9781003369707-2

of mothers, would also help families have the flexibility to cope with a rapidly changing economy, as at least one member of a family should be in employment at any one time. Since there was a change in the nature of risks, argued NSR writers, meeting these new needs would not necessarily require overall increases in public spending. Money that had been spent confronting the old risks could be transferred to dealing with the new ones. The overall result would be an upgrading of the quality of the work force without increased net public cost.

These arguments served three purposes. First, they justified a major role for public spending and public social policy, rebutting neoliberal arguments that public spending was mere waste. Second, it was helpful to reformers in social democratic and other progressive movements to move from their parties away from their old base in the predominantly male old industrial working class and develop policies that would attract workers, and particularly women, in new sectors of the economy. These arguments around NSR and SIWS were fundamental to the 'Third Way' movements of the 1990s associated with such figures as Bill Clinton, Tony Blair, and Gerhard Schröder. Finally, and more substantively, these policies addressed a serious need; the arguments about requirements and opportunities to adjust to the challenges of globalization were well rooted in the evidence of social science (Esping-Andersen 2002).

There were, however, three major problems. First, expectations that the new economy had achieved a level of stability in which the old social risks were no longer serious threats proved to be very misguided. If anything, the increased role of financial markets in that economy has made it highly unstable. The great crisis of 2007–2008 is only the largest example to date of a more general riskiness. Financial traders and wealthy people are able to treat the risks in these markets as opportunities to speculate, hedge their bets, and make money, but ordinary working people with little or no ability to manipulate financial assets bear the brunt of the instability that this causes. After 2008, the old social risks returned with a vengeance, refuting the argument that SIWS policies would not impose extra costs. 'Old' social protection is still very much needed, a need made more intense by the continuing growth of inequality. The very wealthy are taking an increasing share of consumption growth, leaving less to serve as a cushion against uncertainty for the rest of the population (Bastagli et al. 2012; Förster et al. 2014; OECD 2011). People respond by having increasing recourse to consumption credit, which brings the threat of a return of the financial crisis.

A second problem was that the more enthusiastic NSR writers tended to stigmatize 'old' policies of social protection as 'passive', more or less sharing the neoliberal perspective that public spending of this kind represents waste. It must be remembered that the original plans of Rehn and Meidner in Sweden, Beveridge in the United Kingdom, and others did not see programmes of social protection as merely passive; rather they would give workers and their families a sense of security that would help them confront risks in the market with confidence. These arguments were, in fact, very similar to those of advocates of NSR. Further, these programmes operated as automatic stabilizers, enabling workers to continue spending and sustaining consumption during periods of recession.

Finally, SIWS policies are vulnerable to what has become known as the 'Matthew principle'. This refers to the words attributed to Jesus Christ in the parable of the talents in the Gospel of St. Matthew: 'For unto every one that hath shall be given, and he shall have abundance: but from him that hath not shall be taken away even that which he hath' (Matthew 25: 29). As several researches have shown (Cantillon 2011; Bonoli et al. 2017; Van Kersbergen and Kraft 2017), SIWS policies have something of this effect: improved educational opportunities tend to be taken advantage of by people from already prosperous families; skilled workers are more likely to take advantage of retraining opportunities than the less skilled; middle- and higher-income families usually benefit most from family-friendly employment and social policies.

These objections are serious. They may have contributed to a sense of being neglected by public policy among workers in declining areas and sectors who have found it difficult to benefit from the policy shift. Third Way social policies may therefore have contributed to the rising popularity of right-wing extremism. However, countries with a strong social investment approach remain economically successful, with lower levels of inequality than nearly all those that lack such policies – whether these latter be neoliberal cases like the USA and United Kingdom or the poor-quality welfare states of southern and CEE. Although arguments that the SIWS approach has been accompanied by 'Matthew effects' are valid and important, one cannot find counter-factual cases – that is, countries that have ignored SIWS and produced egalitarian societies with high levels of employment and high-value-added products. The answer lies, as Bonoli et al. (2017) argue, in ensuring that SIWS does not substitute for redistributive policies; rather, the more SIWS, the greater the need for a redistributive welfare state.

2.2 SIWS 2.0

These weaknesses do not undermine the central contentions of the SIWS approach, but they have led to a more cautious formulation of what it can achieve. The case for SIWS, as Hemerijck (2012, 2017) and Morel et al. (2012) make clear, rests on the assumption that the economy will continue to create major opportunities for highly educated and skilled people. So far, this has proved to be the case. Over 40 years ago, the Dutch economist Jan Tinbergen (1975) argued that there was a race in the labour market between technology and education: technology tended to destroy low-skilled jobs but to create opportunities for highly skilled ones; the question was whether education could keep pace with the change, producing enough educated and skilled people to take advantage of new up-market possibilities. So far the OECD considers that the race has turned out about even (OECD 2011: chapter 1): the number of jobs using high skills has increased at least as fast as the decline in the unskilled. But this optimism needs three corrections.

First, a certain proportion of low-skilled jobs will always remain. It is the holders of these who suffer the negative consequences that Cantillon (2011) describes. Second, as already mentioned, within the overall up-market move of the advanced economies, there will always be major shock episodes, not just marginal adjustments with which equilibrium can cope, when major firms, industries, and sometimes entire regional economies, collapse. These disturb the orderly adjustments of what Hemerijck (2017) has termed 'stocks, flows and buffers', and should be expected to increase in frequency in the globalizing economy. Eventually, new and better activities should arrive to provide new opportunities in affected areas, but this can be a protracted process. In the meantime a population incurs major insecurity and possibly a move into poverty. This is when right-wing populism becomes a particular risk.

Finally, we cannot assume that the Tinbergen race will continue to turn out so even. At least in some countries and regions, the search for constant upgrading may be unsuccessful. In all these cases, the protective welfare state continues to be necessary, partly to provide passive support but also to give people the confidence to take risks when opportunities do occur, and to continue to consume without a need to take on debt, thereby sustaining consumption.

The renewed SIWS project fully retains the original emphasis on the importance of paid work. It is consistent with the idea that the dignity and political power of people outside a small elite are rooted in the fact that their work is economically useful. This is contested by those who consider that work can be provided for all only under increasingly degraded conditions, and that we should explore such policies as a citizen's income that would enable some people not to work at all (Standing 2014). It is highly unlikely that such an approach would be accepted in a predominantly neoliberal age, but even if it were, it would have negative implications. People dependent on a citizen's income would be highly vulnerable to drastic income loss should the political consensus that introduced it change, as is likely.

Behind this issue stands a more fundamental one: the normative base of citizenship and the relation of SIWS to it (Morel and Palme 2017). SIWS is consistent with the approach to citizenship that sees it, not as an abstract set of entitlements, but as something we enjoy because our society needs us. We contribute our labour power and skill, and it is in exchange for this that we proudly, not gratefully, expect various rights. This 'rights imply responsibilities' approach is sometimes seen as conservative, but this is an error. If rights do not have this kind of basis, they can quickly become seen as privileges that have been granted, whether by a ruling elite or by our fellow citizens, either of whom might decide to remove them. The work-based concept of citizenship is characteristic of Nordic social democracy, but it acquires new importance in highly economic neoliberal societies.

If work has this centrality to citizenship, it becomes a highly important collective good. This is problematic since work requires a base in the market if it is not to become highly inefficiently organized. The collective good cannot be secured by the state just providing jobs or even through Keynesian demand management. The state has to provide the collective goods elements of work by operating alongside the market. For example, it can ensure that its activities do not hinder job creation in the market but instead provide incentives for it. Forms of taxation like employers' contributions to social insurance must not give employers a disincentive to employ labour; contributions need to be based on turnover, not employment. The costs of job security need to be borne by the state rather than by employers, which for southern European countries in particular means a move from employment protection laws (that throw the burden of workers' security on to the employer) to generous publicly funded unemployment support and the SIWS agenda. It might have been acceptable for employment protection to be borne by employers when these were benefitting from protectionist walls maintained by governments, as in the first period of post-war industrial development; but in open labour markets it can become a major hindrance.

Tax credits for people in low-paid work and other elements of the Bonoli et al. (2017) agenda for combating the Matthew principle are also important. These measures too imply a shift in the cost of supporting employment and wages from employers to the state. The point is to facilitate a working population able to compete in open labour markets but with various forms of non-protectionist state support. The normative base of these is citizenship entitlements, not 'welfare handouts'.

This argument implies citizenship rights for those who are preparing to work, who are working, who would work if they were not sick or disabled, or who have worked until they are old. This does not include everybody. Chiara Saraceno (2017) and others have warned of the negative consequences of this approach for parenthood. The pressure to be members of the paid workforce is causing some resentment among women in the Nordic countries who would prefer to be full-time mothers. Traditional Christian, in particular Roman Catholic, social policy has always stressed the value of motherhood, and this has been part of its own distinctive critique of the values of capitalism and the market economy. These values have become unpopular during the current shared neoliberal and social-democratic agenda of eliminating the barriers to women's labour force participation, particularly because it has always been an aspect of male domination. But this does not dispose of a serious argument. It should be possible for individuals and families not to have their lives dominated by the market, including the labour market. This has implications beyond our present concerns, but the place of parents (not just mothers) in the work-based model of citizenship is highly relevant. The SIWS agenda addresses this very directly with its emphasis on childcare but needs to go further (León 2017; Saraceno 2017). Social policy must recognize the right of a parent of pre-school children to be a full-time parent – helping to prepare the next generation of working citizens – and to receive public financial support, even if he or she has a partner in paid employment. Such rights have been recognized for mothers, and the idea of paid parental leave from work for limited periods is beginning to be accepted for fathers too. These policies need to be developed further.

2.3 The political geography of SIWS

It is finally important to examine where, and to what extent, SIWS policies are currently being pursued and whether we can attribute any particular effects to them. Some relevant data are collected by Eurostat and are mainly limited to European Union (EU) member states (at the time of writing, including the United Kingdom) (see also De Deken 2017; Verbist 2017). This partly reflects the fact that major developments in social policy are mainly limited to highly developed welfare states, and these are nearly all to be found only in Europe.

There are three main dimensions to the SIWS: education, reskilling through active labour market policy, and family policy. The first of these is by far the largest. It is of course no new policy area introduced by SIWS thinking, but a bias towards a high level of public spending on education within social policy is central to SIWS. Figure 2.1 depicts levels of public education spending as a proportion of gross domestic product (GDP) among EU member states (plus Norway and Switzerland) for the most recent year available in Eurostat data (2014, for some countries, 2013). It is unfortunately not possible to include Denmark, as public education spending is not calculated on a comparable basis in that country, but it is certainly at the high end of the range. (Greece has also not furnished data to Eurostat for this item.) The other Nordic countries (Sweden, Finland and Norway) and Belgium lead education spending, followed by most north-west European countries. With the exception of the two small islands (Cyprus and Malta), spending in southern and central Europe is much lower, with Italy being among the very lowest. However, the low level of spending in Germany should also be noted. This is partly a distortion resulting from the partly private (business) nature of spending on the German public vocational education system; even larger calculation problems of this kind led to the omission of Denmark altogether from these statistics. However, there is general recognition among German policy makers that education has been a neglected area of public policy in that country.

Even among the low spenders, European public spending on education is higher than that elsewhere. Were the USA to be included in Figure 2.1, it would fall between Poland and Estonia; Japan would come between Italy and the Czech Republic. The US case is partly explained by the high level of private spending on education there, a factor that reinforces the 'Matthew' effect; our concern here is with public policy. We are unable to consider differences in the quality of education, or its helpfulness in the labour market, across different countries; it must be borne in mind that spending data are only approximate indicators of these factors, but simple indicators are needed for comparisons of the kind being attempted here.

Strategies for retraining and reskilling the workforce might appear as part of education spending, but they are largely grouped under 'active labour market policy' (ALMP). 'Passive' labour market policy mainly comprises financial transfers to support the unemployed; 'active' policies are those designed to get them into work. These include

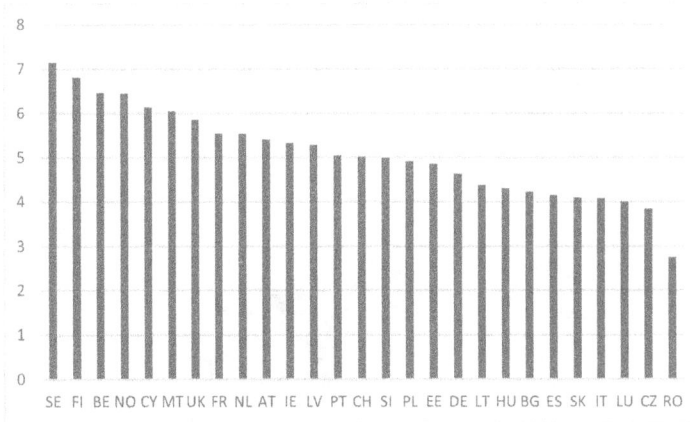

Figure 2.1 Public spending on education as percentage of GDP, European countries, c. 2014

Source: Eurostat

the negative disciplinary approaches known in the USA as 'workfare', based on the assumption that unemployment is caused by voluntary idleness. But ALMP also includes retraining and various measures to help people find work and equip them for it – an approach pioneered in the Nordic countries in the 1960s. In general, the higher the spending on ALMP, the more the policy includes measures of this kind rather than mere workfare, which is in itself cheap.

Figure 2.2 shows spending on ALMP in 2014 or 2013, except for the United Kingdom, where the statistic is for 2010. (The United Kingdom gave up reporting its very low spending on this area of policy in that year.) The data cover all EU member states, but not Norway or Switzerland. In all cases, this spending is of course much lower than that for education, but the pattern is similar, with the Nordic countries (here including Denmark) again leading, with the exception of Norway, and most of north-western Europe (with the striking exceptions of Germany and the United Kingdom) following. With the exception of Hungary, levels in CEE are considerably lower than those in southern Europe.

Finally, Figure 2.3 examines spending on employment-friendly family policies. Here we have data for all EU member states except Belgium; there are no data for Norway and Switzerland. The role of family policy in the SIWS strategy is mainly to facilitate parents (both fathers and mothers) to participate in the labour market. This does not embrace all areas of family policy – in particular, it excludes family allowances, birth payments, and other financial transfers that might be seen as making

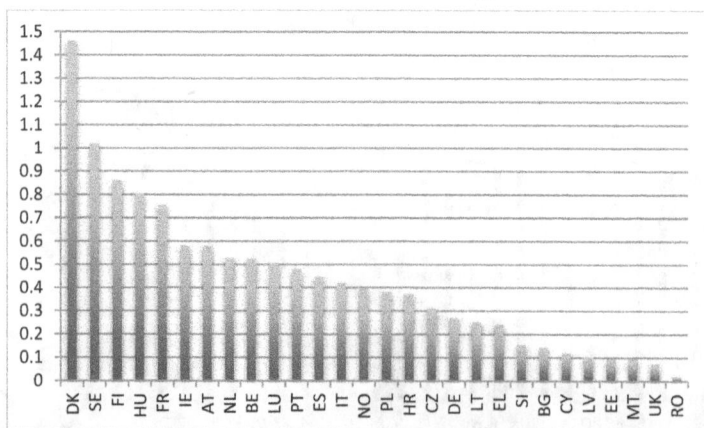

Figure 2.2 Public spending on ALMP as percentage of GDP, European countries, c. 2014

Source: Eurostat

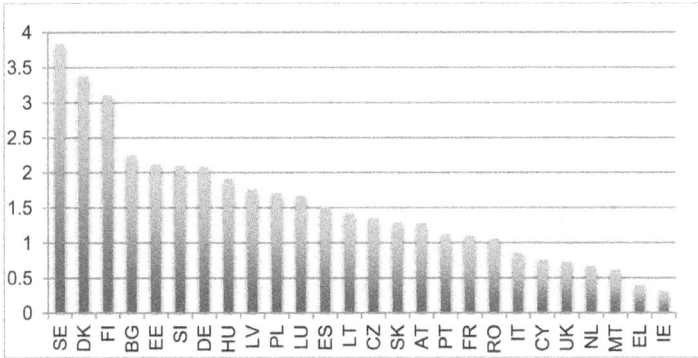

Figure 2.3 Public spending on employment-friendly family policies as percentage of GDP, European countries, c. 2014

Source: Eurostat

it possible for families to manage without such participation. It will include transfers for purposes like parental leave designed to support temporary absences from the labour market, childcare, and pre-school education. These latter two, which constitute most spending in this area, facilitate employment among parents of young children, particularly mothers. Included in Figure 2.3 are those elements of family policy that match the SIWS model.

Again, the Nordic countries dominate, but there is also high spending among many CEE cases, with north-western and southern countries spread in no particular pattern. The strong position of CEE is a continuing legacy from the communist period, when there was a strong emphasis on enabling the mothers of young children to participate in paid employment.

We can combine data for all three elements to provide an overall index of SIWS commitment (Figure 2.4). Since individual components lacked data for different countries, the number of countries left with full results is restricted. The only remaining Nordics, Sweden and Finland, continue to head the list, but after that there is an interesting complexity, with only France and Austria in western Europe spending as much on SIWS policies as several CEE countries.

It is interesting to examine the importance of SIWS spending as a proportion of total public spending, as opposed to proportion of GDP, as this demonstrates the relative importance of SIWS within public spending and policy (Figure 2.5). This further demonstrates the relative importance of SIWS spending in CEE countries. Several of these

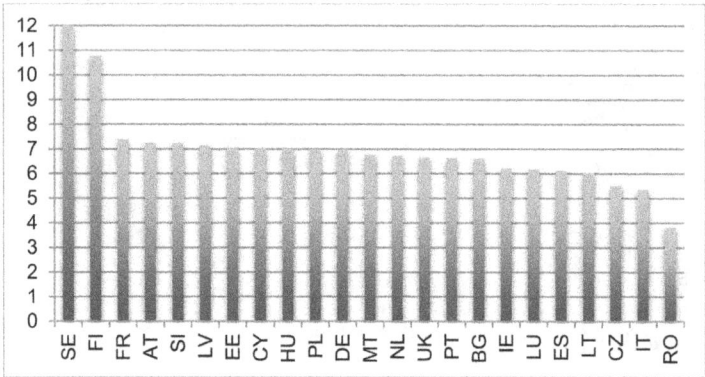

Figure 2.4 Public spending on aggregated SIWS policies as percentage of GDP, European countries, c. 2014

Source: Eurostat

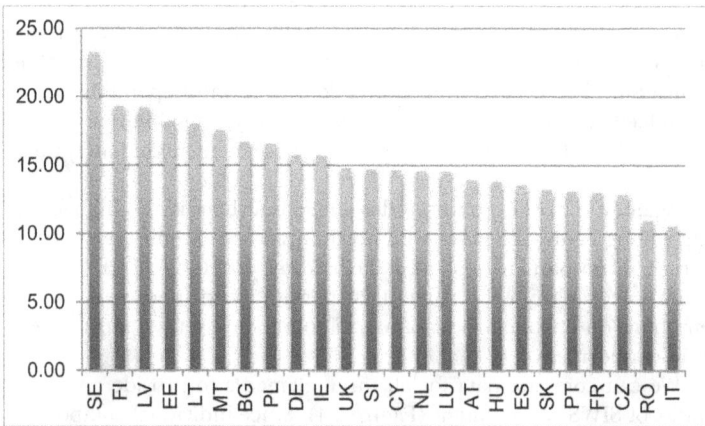

Figure 2.5 Spending on aggregated SIWS policies as percentage of all public spending, European countries, c. 2014

Source: Eurostat

are countries that have not carried over from past times strong commitments to other aspects of public spending, having made a clear break from the strong role for the state in Soviet times. This has left them more free to pursue the relatively new SIWS agenda compared with many western European states.

A major problem with the SIWS strategy is that much of it is for the long term. If a country were to start expanding and improving its education system now, we should not expect to see results for about a decade, though ALMP and family policy might be expected to have quicker results. The main claim made for the strategy is that it enables countries with high wages and other labour costs to remain competitive and provide high levels of employment despite global competition. A reasonable test of its effectiveness would therefore be to check whether the development of SIWS strategies (measured, as before, through public spending) correlates with levels of employment. Figure 2.6 shows the results of setting SIWS spending in c. 2014 with employment levels in 2016. The relationship is positive but not strong: $r^2 = 0.2419$. It certainly should not be expected by even the most enthusiastic supporters of SIWS that it would be the principal factor explaining employment levels, but it is interesting to explore which countries in particular deviate from levels of employment that might be expected if SIWS *were* a major factor. We can do this by first calculating the equation of the hypothetical relationship between SIWS spending and employment level across the countries for which we have full data. This enables us to predict the level of employment that a country would have, were this equation to apply. We then subtract this from the actual employment level in the country concerned, and divide the result by the standard deviation of the employment level across all countries. This indicates how far an individual country deviates from the expected pattern. We shall count

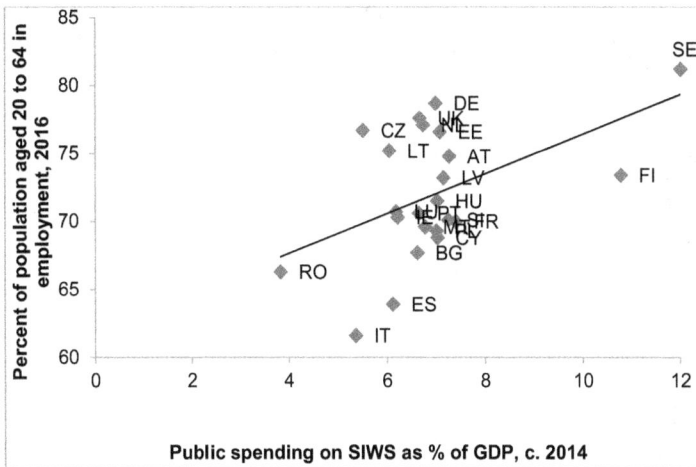

Figure 2.6 Spending on SIWS policies as percentage of GDP, c. 2014 by employment level, 2016, European countries

as exceptional cases those that deviate by more than one standard deviation in either direction.

These calculations produce: countries with higher levels of employment than SIWS would predict: the Czech Republic, Germany, the Netherlands, and the United Kingdom; with lower levels: Italy and Spain. It is notable that in 2016, the German government moved to strong endorsement of the SIWS approach (Bundesfinanzministerium 2016). It argued that the country would not be able to sustain its strong economic performance unless it did more to improve skill levels and make it easier for women to join the labour market. In particular, it was argued that, given Germany's low birth rate, it would need to accept large numbers of immigrants and refugees to sustain the labour force, the latter in particular requiring considerable educational support. The Czech Republic has successfully attracted investment in manufacturing from western Europe, mainly because of its legacy of a strong base from communist times. The United Kingdom has long been seen as pursuing a different path in labour market policy from much of the rest of western Europe, relying on an unregulated labour market to encourage job-creation. Italy and Spain are among those southern European countries that had not adapted their economies to modern employment before the financial crisis and consequent Eurocrisis struck.

There is a considerable difference in the relationship between SIWS and male and female employment. There is no correlation at all with male employment: $r^2 = 0.03886$. But the correlation with female employment is 0.33136. The most significant relationship is between female employment and spending on family policies. While the relationship to employment among both genders is only 0.07294, it is 0.33667 for women's employment (Figure 2.7). This suggests that to date the most

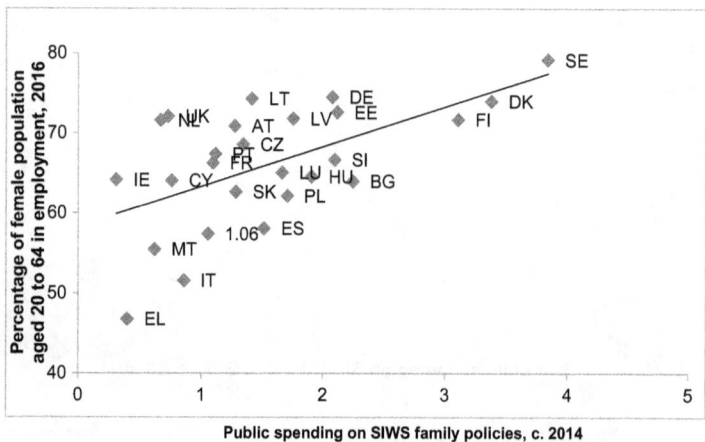

Figure 2.7 Spending on SIWS family policies as percentage of GDP, c. 2014 by female employment level, 2016, European countries

effective impact of SIWS policies is the help afforded to women to enter the paid labour force by supportive family policies. The countries that conform least to the equation (using the calculations set out earlier) are: those with higher female employment than predictable on the basis of family policies: Lithuania, the Netherlands, and the United Kingdom; with lower levels: Greece, Italy, and Spain. Lithuania is a country with a strong legacy of female employment from Soviet days; the Netherlands is notable for having relied on a high level of part-time work among both men and women as its main means for encouraging dual-working families. The United Kingdom, again, has followed its own path. All southern European countries except for Portugal are low performers.

2.4 Conclusions

We can conclude from this analysis that SIWS seems already to be important in facilitating female employment, but it is clearly not the only means available for achieving high employment in general. The experience of the Nordic countries suggests that if a country adopts strong SIWS policies, it can combine a low degree of inequality and a strong welfare state, enabling a large proportion of its population to work in highly skilled, high value-added sectors (the Nordic way). That of the United Kingdom (and probably the USA, not covered in this account) suggests that a strong SIWS is not necessary to achieve high employment for both men and women, but is this at the price of higher inequality? That is a question for future research.

There are clearly different paths towards sustaining strong labour markets; SIWS does not provide the 'single best way', but it is an available strategy for countries that have a need to move out of a trap of competition on price alone – which brings with it low wages and specialisms in low-value-added activities. This choice may be particularly important for southern European countries. With the exception of some sectors and regions in Italy and Spain, until about 25 years ago, these countries found their main niches as the low-cost suppliers of textiles, cheap clothing and white goods to the rest of western Europe. During the 1990s, that role became unavailable. The Multifibre Agreement brought to an end tariffs erected by the advanced economies against textiles and clothing from the Far East; and the entry of CEE countries into the capitalist economy gave western Europe and the rest of the world access to some low-cost but highly skilled workers. Southern Europe lost its old role. Its countries now face the choice of either reducing their living standards until they can compete on price with CEE or raising the quality of their products and production methods until they join the ranks of high-value-added producers. Again, some sectors and regions in Italy and Spain are doing this, but not their national economies as a whole.

In some respects, workers in the stronger CEE economies – the Czech Republic, Slovakia, and Slovenia – are better placed than their southern European neighbours. While their incomes are low and public services poor, these are improving. And, lacking the inheritance of strong public spending commitments to pensions and social protection of most western European economies, their governments are more easily able to adopt parts of the SIWS agenda. Is it possible for any country to increase its spending on SIWS issues while still burdened with austerity and without betraying social protection commitments from the past? It is relatively easy for Germany, with its disciplined public finances, to begin now to increase its SIWS activities; it is far more difficult for Italy, Spain, and especially Greece.

Appendix: Country name abbreviations

AT Austria
BE Belgium
BG Bulgaria
CH Switzerland
CY Cyprus
CZ Czech Republic
DE Germany
DK Denmark
EE Estonia
EL Greece
ES Spain
FI Finland
FR France
HU Hungary
IE Ireland
IT Italy
LT Lithuania
LU Luxembourg
LV Latvia
MT Malta
NL Netherlands
NO Norway
PL Poland
PT Portugal
RO Romania
SE Sweden
SI Slovenia
SK Slovakia
UK United Kingdom

References

Bastagli, F., Coady, D., Gupta, S. (2012) *Income Inequality and Fiscal Policy* (IMF Staff Discussion Note SDN/12/08). Washington, DC: IMF.

Beck, U. (1986) *Risikogesellschaft.* Frankfurt am Main: Suhrkamp.

Bonoli, G., Cantillon, B., Van Lancker, W. (2017) Social investment and the Matthew effect: Limits to a strategy. In: *The Uses of Social Investment.* Oxford: Oxford University Press, pp. 66–76.

Bundesfinanzministerium. (2016) *Der Vierte Tragfähigkeitsbericht des BFM*. Berlin: BFM.

Cantillon, B. (2011) The paradox of the social investment state: Growth, employment and poverty in the Lisbon era. *Journal of European Social Policy*, 21(5), pp. 432–449.

De Deken, J. (2017) Conceptualizing and measuring social investment. In: Hemerijck, A (ed) *The Uses of Social Investment*. Oxford: Oxford University Press, pp. 184–93.

Esping-Andersen, G., Hemerijck A.E., Gallie, D.E., Myles J. (eds) (2002) *Why We Need a New Welfare State*. Oxford: Oxford University Press.

Ferrera, M. (1998) *Le Trapolle del Welfare*. Bologna: Il Mulino.

Förster, M., Llena-Nozal, A., Nafilyan, V. (2014) *Trends in Top Incomes and Their Taxation in OECD Countries* (OECD Society, Employment and Migration Working Papers 159). Paris: OECD.

Giddens, A. (1994) *Beyond Left and Right. The Future of Radical Politics*. Cambridge: Polity Press.

Giddens, A. (1998) *The Third Way: The Renewal of Social Democracy*. Cambridge: Polity Press.

Hemerijck, A. (2012) *Changing Welfare States*. Oxford: Oxford University Press.

Hemerijck, A. (eds) (2017) *The Uses of Social Investment*. Oxford: Oxford University Press.

León, M. (2017) Social investment and childcare expansion: A perfect match? In Hemerijck, A. (eds) *The Uses of Social Investment*. Oxford: Oxford University Press, pp. 118–27.

Morel, N., Palier, B., Palme, J. (eds) (2012) *Towards a Social Investment Welfare State?* Bristol: Policy Press.

Morel, N., Palme, J. (2017) A normative foundation for the social investment approach? In Hemerijck, A. (eds) *The Uses of Social Investment*. Oxford: Oxford University Press, pp. 150–159.

OECD (2011) *Divided We Stand: Why Inequality Keeps Rising*. Paris: OECD.

Saraceno, C. (2017) Family relationships and gender equality in the social investment discourse: An overly reductive view? In: Hemerijck, A. (eds) *The Uses of Social Investment*. Oxford: Oxford University Press, pp. 59–65.

Standing, G. (2014) *A Precariat Charter: From Denizens to Citizens*. London: Bloomsbury Academic.

Taylor-Gooby, P. (eds) (2004) *New Risks, New Welfare. The Transformation of the European Welfare State*. Oxford: Oxford University Press.

Tinbergen, J. (1975) *Income Distribution: Analysis and Policies*. Amsterdam: North Holland Publishing Co.

Van Kersbergen, K., Kraft, J. (2017) De-universalization and selective social investment in Scandinavia? In Hemerijck, A. (eds) *The Uses of Social Investment*. Oxford: Oxford University Press, pp. 216–26.

Verbist, G. (2017) Measuring social investment returns: Do publicly provided services enhance social inclusion? In Hemerijck, A. (eds) *The Uses of Social Investment*. Oxford: Oxford University Press, pp. 194–205.

3   Minimum income and active labour market policies

The traps of the work-first approaches

Andrea Ciarini, Silvia Girardi, and Valeria Pulignano

3.1 Anti-poverty policies, minimum income, and working poor

In recent years, anti-poverty policies have been at the centre of profound change. As a result of the crisis and the increased number of working poor, that is, those workers who, despite being employed, have a household income below a defined poverty line (Barbieri et al. 2018; Cantillon et al. 2020), every European country, including most recently Greece and Italy, has deployed a wide variety of policy tools to strengthen this pillar of welfare supply: minimum income schemes, as means-tested income support anti-poverty schemes, tax credits and in-work benefits aimed at increasing work incentives for low-income workers and their families, active labour market policies, as well as dedicated social services (housing, education, childcare, and healthcare) to facilitate social inclusion. The 2008–2009 crisis has accelerated these changes. As many authors have emphasised (Vesan and Pavolini 2018; Barbieri et al. 2018), the unprecedented stress on Europe's welfare systems, especially in the Mediterranean countries most affected by the economic and sovereign debt crisis, has had two major consequences. On the one hand, many governments reacted to the first employment shock in 2008–2009, either with traditional measures, such as unemployment benefits, or by extending the coverage of the minimum income schemes (Barbieri et al. 2018).

As a consequence of these reforms, all European countries can now rely on an extended social safety net to fight poverty and social exclusion. However, these readjustments were not without trade-offs. In fact, several authors highlighted that in the medium term, while the number of beneficiaries has been steadily on the rise, means-testing, controls and work conditionalities have been strongly reinforced (Marchal and Van Mechelen 2017), with a marked pressure to favour work at any cost, even at the price of precarious or low-paid employment. Compared to

DOI: 10.4324/9781003369707-3

an early historical phase in which the minimum income schemes were mainly conceived as a passive measure to support the poor, over the years they have been turned into an active tool to support the social and labour reintegration of welfare recipients and also to supplement the incomes of the working poor. Due to the various cycles of reforms that affected anti-poverty policies, there is no doubt that currently different policy tools are involved in this area of social intervention, not only cash benefits to fight social exclusion as in the past but also active labour market policies, fscal welfare, and even the minimum legal wage, where present. These are, however, quite different policy tools. The minimum income is a means tested benefit against poverty, whose amount is generally equal to the difference between the income received within the household, including transfers from other social interventions (e.g. unemployment benefits), and the poverty threshold set by public authorities. These characteristics mark the difference with other instrument supporting income, such as the unemployment benefits and the minimum wage. The former follow an insurance criteria, since they are basically financed by social contribution paid by workers and employers (not by general taxation as in the case of anti-poverty policies), and generally have the function of stabilising the worker's income during the transition from one job to another. The latter is not a cash transfer, but a minimum wage level defined by law, below which no worker may fall. The minimum wage itself is not included in the measures to mitigate poverty, as its main objective is to prevent the wages of low-paid workers from decreasing too much (Barieri et al. 2018). Some authors argue that the minimum legal wage can reduce the need for in-work benefits. (Immervoll and Pearson 2009; Collado et al. 2016). The minimum wage may also be useful in some cases to discourage the use of the minimum income as a wage replacement for the working poor. As it is possible to combine two sources of income, one from work, the other from the minimum income, there may be implicit incentives for employers to reduce their wage bill if part of the wage is supplemented by social assistance, trough minimum income or in-work benefits. In this case, the presence of a minimum wage discourages this option. On the other hand, according to Murray (1990), if the level of the minimum income exceeds that of the minimum wage, there might be a risk of discouraging employment, that is, the choice to participate in the labour market, thus increasing the 'dependency trap' that social policies should clearly address. It must be said that this scenario – that is, benefit dependency – is very unlikely to occur, as minimum wage levels are well above the minimum income in all countries with such measures. In contrast, the opposite risk is much more real – at least if we look at some of the reforms that have been introduced in more recent years, even before the crisis. In order to maintain the incentive for paid work as wages fall, in many cases the minimum wage has been lowered – for example, through cuts or non-indexed benefits (Cantillon et al. 2020). Indeed, reforms that play on incentives to work are based on economic – and we might also say moral – reasoning, according to which people decide to work or not based on economic convenience. According to this logic, welfare must focus on changing the behaviour of the beneficiaries rather than addressing the structural causes of low wages. However, in the case of poverty and social exclusion, the issue of dependency is mainly due to health and social conditions of the beneficiaries and to the lack of adequate job opportunities – not simply to individual aptitudes as in the conservative tradition (Murray 1990).

In this chapter, we focus on these transformations in a selected group of European countries: Germany, France, Denmark, and Italy, representative of different welfare regimes (Continental, Nordic, and Mediterranean) and different traditions of welfare measures against poverty. France and Denmark are among the European countries with the highest social spending and a traditionally generous anti-poverty policy system that has, however, been subject to severe reforms in recent years, especially in Denmark. In Germany, social spending on policy against poverty has increased in recent years, though it remains low in comparison to France and Denmark. More in general the German reforms (in particular the Hartz reforms of 2003–2005) were aimed at strengthening the coverage of minimum income schemes, with however a strong emphasis on a work-first approach which completely reversed the previous system of both unemployment benefits and social assistance for the poor. In this framework, Italy is a country that has traditionally lacked a dedicated social safety net against poverty, at least until the more recent years. In fact, most recent reforms (Reddito di Inclusione and Reddito di Cittadinanza) have radically changed the system of policies against the poverty, with an unprecedented increase in both public spending and beneficiaries. The chapter is organised as follows: Section 3.2 provides an overview of the reforms most recently introduced in the four countries analysed. In Section 3.3, the focus is on active measures associated with minimum income schemes. From there, in Section 3.4, we will address the issue of community work as a condition to access the benefit. In Section 3.5, we will come to general conclusions based on the analysis.

3.2 Policies against poverty in in Germany, Denmark, France, and Italy: a summary

The countries we have chosen for benchmarking represent a fairly wide variety of national anti-poverty and activation models.

If we look at the evolution over time, common changes in trends emerge. Although coming from different starting points, all countries

Table 3.1 Expenditure and generosity of anti-poverty policies in Denmark, France, Germany, and Italy, Year 2020

	Denmark	France	Germany	Italy
Total expenditure as a percentage of GDP	1.3 (2019)	0.5	0.1	0.4
Beneficiaries as a percentage of the population	3.52	3	4.7	4.7
Beneficiaries as a percentage of the population at risk of poverty or social exclusion	20.6	17	23	19
People at risk of poverty or social exclusion as a percentage of total population	16.8	18.9	20.4	24.9

Source: Author's elaboration from the national statistical offices and the Eurostat online database.

suffer from decreasing ability to combat poverty, resulting in an increase in the incidence of in-work poverty (see Figures 3.1 and 3.2). This is particularly true for countries that, unlike Italy, can count on a well-structured policy system that has evolved over time. Denmark remains among the European countries with the highest redistributive policy system in Europe, both in terms of beneficiaries and impact of transfer on poverty reduction. However, the capacity to tackling poverty is increasingly diminishing also in this country (see again Figure 3.1). In parallel, despite being still below the EU average, in-work poverty is on the rise (see Figure 3.2; see also Larsen 2017).

Indeed, the succession of welfare state reforms in Denmark from the year 2000 to the present day have moved in the direction of increasingly restrictive and conditional access to minimum income, and the changes are to the detriment of specific social groups such as young people, larger families, and those who cannot prove long-term residence in the country. In particular, major reforms have led to reduced benefits for these social groups and increasing conditionality in terms of stricter work conditionalities requirements and controls, as well as to the detriment of training opportunities (Hansen 2019).

To date, the minimum income falls into three channels of income support: the Kontjaentjhaelp (the basic scheme), the resourceforlobsydelse (for those who are unable to work due to complex social problems), and the uddannelseshjaelp (for young people under 30). In 2015, a fourth one was added – the *integrationsydelse* – for those who cannot prove they have been residents for at least seven of the eight previous years, whether they are Danish, EU, or non-EU citizens.

These four channels of support differ in their underlying activation logic and in the degree of financial support. The last two provide

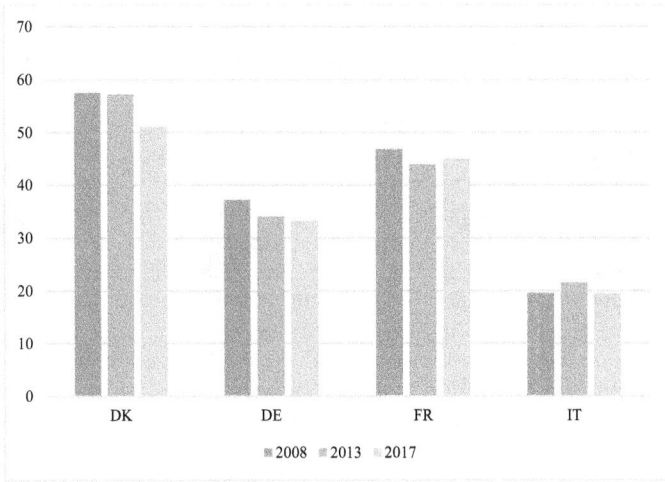

Figure 3.1 Impact of transfers, excluding pensions, on poverty reduction, Val. %, Years 2008–2017

Source: Author's elaboration from the Eurostat online database

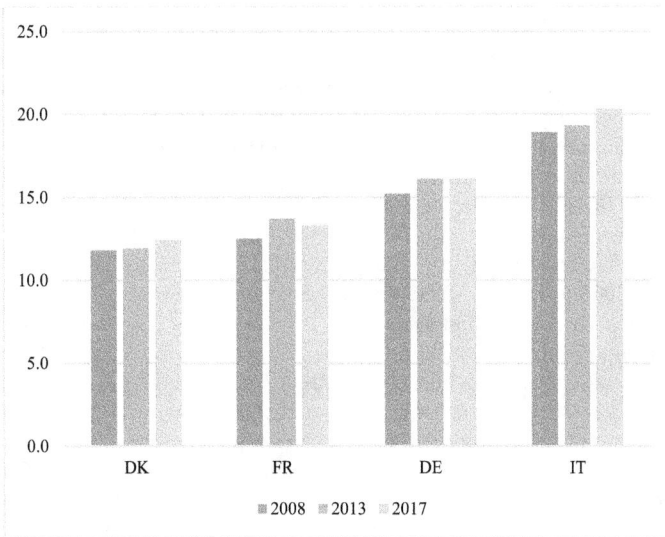

Figure 3.2 The incidence of in-work poverty, Val. %, Years 2008–2017

Source: Author's elaboration from the Eurostat online database

reduced benefits, amounting to about half of those guaranteed for the first two. Although the levels of social protection offered by the minimum income are comparatively high in the European context for those citizens who have access to the full amount, this is not the case for those population groups (young people, residents for less than seven years, and those who cannot prove a 225-day work record for the previous year) who are only entitled to receive half the amount. This amount is considered insufficient to meet basic needs for living a life in compliance with the standards calculated by methods such as reference budgets (Larsen 2017). Moreover, the consequences of these restrictive changes are to be understood in a broader context of reforms that affected the level of social protection afforded by other income support measures such as disability and invalidity pensions and unemployment benefits. Social security reforms introduced in 2010 also limited access to and the duration of these income support measures. In 2013, the duration of unemployment benefits was shortened from four to two years, and access criteria became more restrictive. In addition, sickness benefits were reduced to five months (compared to former coverage, which was meant to last until the person was able to work again or until retirement), and access to disability benefits approaching the level of the minimum income guarantee was made impossible for people under the age of 40.

On the other hand, changes in conditionality seem to have lost track of the purpose of the minimum income guarantee which is to provide support to those who cannot support themselves. In a way, it is as if the reforms reduced the beneficiaries to a group of unemployed and jobseekers who have to find autonomy through work without taking into account illnesses and accidents that might lead to temporary or permanent disabilities preventing them from working. This paradigm shift focuses policies on the issue of unemployment rather than lack of income.

A closer look shows the same philosophy underpins the Hartz reforms that redesigned the income protection system in Germany between 2003 and 2005, when the tax-based unemployment benefit was unified with the residual social assistance measures provided by local authorities (Socialhilfe). With the Hartz IV reforms, the previous three-level income protection system (insurance benefit, unemployment benefit, and social assistance) has been reduced to only two: on the one hand, the insurance benefit paid by social contribution, and, on the other, the new minimum income scheme, as a dedicated social assistance measure available not only for jobseekers and unemployed persons but also for low-income workers (Eichhorst and Marx 2009). In this case, the new minimum income works as an in-work benefit aimed at increasing employment incentives for disadvantaged groups, while remaining in, or taking up, low-paid work.

Before the Hartz IV reform, unemployment benefits were paid without any means-testing, with a maximum duration of between 6 and 32 months. At the end of this period, the unemployed could benefit from a means-tested tax-based social assistance provided by local authorities without time limits. Starting from 2005, unemployment assistance and social assistance were combined into a single new means-tested benefit, at a return level that is similar to that of the previous Socialhilfe. Since its establishment, the resources transferred by the minimum income scheme (Arbeitslosengeld II) to the beneficiaries take into account certain requirements that de facto delimit a range of means-tested interventions strongly oriented to favour, as much as possible, active participation in the labour market, especially for those beneficiaries that were previously covered by social assistance. The amount of the minimum income is benchmarked to the consumption expenditure standards of the 15% of households with the lowest income. In 2012, this ratio was lowered by five percentage points (previously 20%), thus further limiting the amount of per capita resources transferred to people at risk of poverty. Access to the benefit also depends on the savings and income of the partner but is open-ended. In this framework, Arbeitslosengeld II guarantees a lump-sum transfer, with tax deductions based on income received and family wealth that aim to increase the resources available to beneficiaries: 20% for incomes between one hundred and 1000 euros and 10% for incomes between 1001 and 1200 euros (Emin 2015). Specific tax exemptions and asset deductions are also provided for each dependent child according to their age (ibid). In addition, beneficiaries may receive, under certain conditions, financial contributions for the payment of medical expenses, housing, and children's school expenses.

Compared to the past, returns are lower, with a lump-sum transfer instead of a return linked to the former wages, and the number of beneficiaries has steadily grown, of whom a large part employed in precarious and low-paid jobs at the margin of the labour market (Eichhorst and Marx 2009; Eichhorst and Hassel 2018). In addition, insurance benefits for core workers have also been revised downwards, with returns revised to 60% of previous income, or 67% in the case of dependent children under 18. There has also been a period of eligibility limited to one year compared to the previous 32 months, though this is extendable to two if the person has been working for at least two years continuously, or with an 18-month extension in the case of people over 55.

It is interesting to compare this process with what was done during the same period in France. While the Hartz reforms between 2003 and 2005 represented a profound change, France adhered to its past patterns, without much altering the previous income protection system. This was not only due to the higher level of social spending, which remained higher compared to Germany, but also due to the persistence of a three-tier system: insurance benefits, tax-based unemployment benefits, and minimum income for those excluded from the Bismarckian pillars. In terms of expenditure and the number of users, the main mean policy against poverty is the RSA, set up in 2009 to replace two previous social assistance benefits, the Revenu Minimum d'Insertion (RMI) – already present since the 1980s – and the Allocation de Parent Isolé (API), a previous form of welfare transfer for lone parent families. RSA alone covers almost 50% of the users of the so-called minima sociaux with an expenditure of about €12 billion euros per year – €11.622 billion in 2019 (Drees 2021). There are nine groups of minimum income schemes, plus one specifically for asylum seekers. Four of the schemes – Revenu de Solidarité Active socle (RSA), Allocation aux Adultes Handicapés (AAH), Minimum Vieillesse, and Allocation de Solidarité Spécifique (ASS), absorb 97% of the dedicated resources, with a total expenditure of €27.468 billion in 2021 (ivi). Although aimed at different categories of users, these policies are all non-contributory, that is they are financed from tax revenue, and are means tested, with eligibility linked to income and any other form of revenue available to potential users, from financial assets such as land rents to any form of assistance already provided by the state. Moreover, with the exception of the Allocation de Solidarité aux Personnes Agées (ASPA), a welfare measure for over-65s excluded from social health insurance, that is, provided by the national health service, and financed through social contributions, all remaining measures are targeted at working-age people. According to data from Drees (2021), in 2020, the nine Minima Sociaux institutions reached around 5.5 million people, including family members of individual beneficiaries. The main Minima Sociaux working as a minimum income scheme is the RSA. It was introduced in 2009 to integrate three previous minimum income schemes and tax credit for low income working families, the Revenu Minimum d'Insertion (RMI) – the first guaranteed minimum income introduced in Europe – and the Allocation de Parent Isolé (API) – a previous single-parent family benefits. Like other minimum income devoted to fight poverty, while promoting active labour market participation, the RSA have a double aim: on the hand to alleviate poverty, and on the other, to help beneficiaries to enter the labour market. Since its introduction, it has been reformed several times, with the aim of encouraging active inclusion in the labour market. The initial reform was based on two main pillars: the RSA-Socle, targeting beneficiaries with no work activities, and the RSA-Activité, which targeted low-income working people (Vlandas 2013). The Goal of the RSA-Activitè was to top-up the earned income of low-income families, working as a tax credit. In addition, the Prime pour l'Emploi, worked as an additional tax credit for single low-paid workers. Over the years, various work incentive measures have been introduced alongside transfers to combat poverty. In 2016, the RSA-Activitè and the Prime pour l'Emploi were merged in a single in-work benefit, the Prime Activité, which currently works as an in-work benefit paid to low-income working people, including beneficiaries of RSA.

Finally, in the case of Italy, it did not for a long time have actual anti-poverty policies, in the sense of policy tools specifically dedicated to those excluded from the labour market and to the unemployed who had exhausted the insurance protections. In parallel, Italy has been one of the European countries where poverty and social exclusion have spread the most in the more recent years, as a consequence of the deterioration of the labour market and the limitations of welfare provisions (Barbieri et al. 2018; Natili 2017; Ciarini and Rizza 2021; Saraceno et al. 2020). In a context traditionally marked by the considerable segmentation of the labour market, with significant differences existing between core and peripheral workers, together with social policies' limited capacity to reduce the poverty rate (compared to the other major European countries), the increase in social inequality has had significant effects on the welfare state. The weakness of those social policies designed to combat poverty reflects a persistent passive imbalance in the Italian welfare system's spending (in particular in terms of social security provisions). Against this background, poverty and social exclusion became one of the most relevant topics of political debate following the outbreak of the economic crisis. Indeed, prior to the 2008 crisis, this kind of reform was only of modest interest within the socio-political debate. It was only when the levels of poverty and social exclusion rose dramatically, that renewed pressure emerged for the introduction of a specific reform, which began to influence the political agenda. In an unprecedented effort, between 2017 and 2019, Italy completely revised its policy to combat poverty. In just two years, two different reforms completely reshaped the landscape of Italian antipoverty policies.

The establishment of the Inclusion Income (Reddito di Inclusione) in 2017 marked a first important change in Italy's anti-poverty measures. One strongpoint of the Inclusion Income was undoubtedly its attempt to go beyond the lengthy series of experimental and indiscriminate measures that had characterised the previous years. The financial commitment, while of a substantial nature compared to the past (2 billion euros compared to 750 million spent on previous provisions), nevertheless remains below requirements in view of the significant increase in the risk of poverty. From a comparative perspective, the Inclusion Income remained a rather ungenerous measure, with the maximum amounts payable ranging from 168 euros for an individual, to 485 euros for large families, and is not sufficient to cover all of those living in absolute poverty in Italy. Nevertheless, the increase in spending it implied was significantly more than that of previous reforms. With the introduction of the Citizenship Income (Reddito di Cittadinanza), together with the Citizenship Pension, spending on measures designed to combat poverty (5.9 billion euros in 2019, 7.1 billion in 2020, and 7.2 billion as of 2022) reached levels comparable to those of the other principal European countries. The number of beneficiaries increased in an unprecedented manner, rising from 1.8 million to around 4 million, which is near the number of individuals living in absolute poverty in 2017 (Sacchi and Gallo 2019). Since its introduction, 2.2 million households, corresponding to 4.8 million people, have benefited from the (INPS 2022). The new economic benefit consists of two components: the first component – 'income' – is calculated on the basis of a family's income, which must be below 6,000 euros (or 7,560 euros in the case of the Citizenship Income scheme), multiplied by a corresponding equivalence scale that increases the amounts. The second component of Citizenship Income consists in the reimbursement of rents paid (up to a maximum of 3,360 euros a year) or mortgage payments made (up to 1,800 euros a year). The overall entity of this benefit cannot exceed 9,360 euros per year (780 euros a month) multiplied by the equivalence scale, less the amount of a family's actual income.

In terms of poverty reduction, the Reddito di Cittadinanza has strengthened those social policies designed to combat poverty and social exclusion. Compared to the Inclusion Income, it undoubtedly marks a step forward in the fight against absolute poverty. The data released by the Italian National Statistics Institute (Istat 2020) indicate that since its introduction, the Reddito di Cittadinanza reduced the number of families living in absolute poverty by 148,000 in 2019. Other data (Inps 2020) highlight how, thanks to this measure, the intensity of poverty has decreased, with positive effects on the fight against inequality – since its introduction, the gini index has fallen from 33.9% to 33.2%. More recent data by the Italian National Institute of Statistics (2022) indicates that thanks to the RdC and other emergency measures to tackle the pandemic crisis, one million people (corresponding to 500,000 households) avoided falling into absolute poverty in 2020.

In this regard, while the impact of the RdC in terms of poverty reduction is unquestionable, many authors have criticised the introduction of an equivalence scale that favours single beneficiaries while penalising large families. In fact, while unprecedented funds have been allocated to single-member households (up to 780 euros per month), large families have been penalised. Other concerns regard the lack of a close synergy between minimum income and dedicated social services related to health, care, and work-life balance; schooling for minors also needs to be highlighted. These are all generally included in several minimum income measures, even those that prioritise work-first, such as the German Hartz IV.

3.3 Active labour market policies and poverty reduction

As mentioned at the beginning, several studies of minimum income point out how these institutions have tightened their access criteria and activation conditionality over the years (Marchal and Van Mechelen 2017). At the same time, beneficiaries have also become increasingly heterogeneous and include a large part of working poor. Germany is a typical example of this shift. As a result of the Hartz reforms, over the years, fewer beneficiaries now draw unemployment benefit, and more are now in employment, albeit in low-wage jobs, even if subsidised by the minimum income. There is the well-known case of mini-jobs, which pay a maximum of 450 euros per month, including limited tax and social security payments contributed by employers. Already in place since the 1970s as contractual forms aimed at regularising irregular work, mostly at home, mini-jobs were de facto liberalised with the Hartz reforms, reaching the remarkable figure of 7.6 million in 2016, up from 6 million in 2003 (Schmid 2018). From the perspective of income received, the minimum income can also be used to supplement low incomes from regular work. As highlighted by Alber and Heisig (2011), before the Hartz IV reform, there were about 150,000 people combining social assistance with low income. Afterwards, between 2005 and 2010, their number grew steadily to 1.4 million. This represents 29% of all minimum income recipients.

Together with interventions that also affected the core sectors of the labour market: reduction of unemployment benefits, contractual derogations, and wage restraints (Baccaro and Benassi 2014), mini-jobs, were an essential part of the Hartz reform plan, credited in particular for their contribution to the creation of new jobs, albeit at low wages (Eichhorst and Marx 2012; Ciarini 2016). Inactivity and passive reliance on benefits have certainly been reduced. However, there was also a dark side, the controversial effects of which emerged in the following years. The traditional minimum incomes were based on a reasonable declaration of a person's willingness to be available for work and contained broad exceptions for specific categories (e.g. family conditions – single mothers, people with physical or mental disabilities, people close to retirement age). With the introduction of the Hartz IV, the means by which people are supported or forced to participate in the labour market changed. These policies also extended conditionality to those groups that were previously exempt. In Germany, the direct effect of this shift was certainly an increase in the number of people active in the labour market, but also an increase in low-paid jobs and in-work poverty. It is no coincidence that in 2015 the legal minimum wage was established. At the time, it was set at €8.5, a level lower, for example, than the

French SMIC of about €10 per hour. It was a real novelty for the German industrial relations system, which is traditionally against the use of such instruments. This brings us to active labour market policies. In terms of activation requirements, the Hartz reforms have strongly reinforced the contractual benefits system. The beneficiary is required to prove that he/she is actively looking for a job; otherwise, penalties can vary from 30% to 100% of the subsidy. Unlike other countries, which have also tightened the conditionalities, the unemployed are required to accept any job offer or at least to participate in job-seeking programmes. From this point of view, the emerging system shares features typical of Anglo-Saxon workfare programmes, which exert strong pressure on the unemployed and first-time jobseekers to get into the labour market quickly. As of January 2023, Arbeitslosengeld II will be replaced by a new subsidy, the Bürgergeld, as agreed by the coalition government. Compared to the past, this is a reform that aims to soften the sanctions and punitive approach of active labour market policies. The reform aims to remove the obligation to accept whatever temporary employment is offered, investing more in training and the search for job opportunities more in line with the possibilities and aptitudes of the beneficiaries. In light of a 2019 Constitutional Court ruling, penalties for non-compliance will not be allowed to exceed 30% of the monthly allowance and will no longer be able to cover either housing or heating contributions. Another cornerstone of the reform is the six-month period within which monetary benefits may not be reduced and the exclusion of the first two years of assets (up to 60,000 euros, plus 30,000 for each other component) in the computation of the benefit. The basic allowances, as well as the supplements for dependent children will be increased, as will the adjustment for inflation, which is intended to be faster than the delays, even more than a year and a half, that currently burden the payments.

Pressures towards work-first approaches have also affected countries such as France and Denmark, traditionally characterised by systems that are not only more generous but also less conditional. Denmark had first strengthened activation obligations at the end of the 1990s, going on to define appropriate work more comprehensively, and put more pressure on young people under 30 to actively look for work. However, activation policies continued to have an enabling character during that time, that is, they were conceived as measures designed to provide beneficiaries with personalised support for their social and professional inclusion, in terms of counselling or training. In the following years, between 2002 and 2009, a first wave of reforms changed the income support model. In 2002, the introduction of Start Help replaced, and changed the basis of the Social Bistand in force since 1974. The new scheme provides less generous support for those who have not lived in Denmark or the EU for at least 7 of the previous 8 years; it caps the maximum social assistance benefit (effectively reducing housing allowances) and abolishes the definition of adequate activation, which means that any proposed activation measure is considered adequate. In 2005, a further reform again changed the name of minimum income to Kontanthjaelp and tightened its conditionalities, transforming the logic of activation from enabling, to compulsory participation in workfare in order to receive benefits. Participation in activation programmes is very high. In 2014, about 2/3 of the beneficiaries joined one of the programmes (Kvist 2015). They differ from each other only in the underlying activation logic and in the amount of financial support. The two latter, based on a logic of demographic age and residence in the country, involve a reduced benefit amounting to about half of the standard benefit. The aim of the reduction is to encourage the participation of these two social groups in the labour market, even if, in the case of the youth scheme, the idea is also to support their employment and training/education. Although for young people there is still a logic of activation as an investment in human capital, they are also compelled to accept workfare logic in the months prior to the start of a training course or if they cannot find a job by themselves. In these cases, they are asked to take part in community service work (nytteindsats) as a necessary condition for remaining eligible for minimum income. The latest changes introduced in 2016 further tighten conditionality by introducing a new requirement related to work activity engagement. The requirement of a minimum of 225 hours worked in the previous year becomes a condition for maintaining entitlement to the full subsidy, and failure to meet this requirement results in its reduction by about half of the full subsidy.

In a context where the priority becomes short-term labour participation rather than investment in training and education, activation policies become instruments of labour coercion rather than opportunities for development. The Danish case clearly shows how work support has increasingly become an offer that cannot be refused (Lodemel and Trickey 2001). Several authors have classified these changes that have taken place in the Danish activation framework as a shift from a 'make work pay' (Natili 2018) to a 'work-first' approach (Diop-Christensen 2018).

Many of the reforms that have marked the French minima sociaux can be interpreted following the same trend. On the one hand, further work incentives, such as the Prime Activité, have been introduced to make it more convenient to cumulate a subsidy and a (low-paid) job. On the other hand, job search conditionalities and sanctions have been reinforced with the introduction of the Projet Personnalisé d'Accès à l'Emploi (PPAE). The contract between the beneficiaries and the administration (the Pole Emploi) provides for an integrated approach, including skills assessment, training, and employment assistance within a time frame ranging from three months to more than a year. After three months, a job offer is considered reasonable if it is compatible with the professional skills possessed and if it pays at least 95% of the previous salary. Then, after six months, the replacement rate is raised to 85% of the previous salary, with additional rules on the distance between the workers' residence and their workplace. The offer is adjudged to be reasonable when it is located within a radius of 30 km and no more than one hour from the user's home. Finally, the long-term unemployed, that is, those who have been unemployed for more than one year, are obliged to accept a job offer if the expected remuneration is at least higher than the benefits, but in line with acquired skills, and no more than 30 km from home, as is the case after six months.

The mix of rights and duties established by the PPAE foresees sanctions in cases of: unjustified refusal according to the contract established between the beneficiary and the administration; refusal without legitimate reason to follow the training and job search actions also provided for by the PPAE; finally, two consecutive refusals, with no legitimate reason of a reasonable job offer. A report by Drees (2017) on the employment of Minima Sociaux beneficiaries confirmed the persistence of structural weaknesses in job placement policies. These include the high rate of fixed-term jobs, which employ a quarter of the total number of beneficiaries, compared to just under 10% of the overall number of employees, and the low quality of incentivised work, mainly in the lower tertiary sector, including the care sector. It is a fact that personal services have long been considered a type of work specifically appropriate to bring the unemployed and beneficiaries of the Minima Sociaux back into work (see also Chapter 4 by Ciarini).

In Italy, the recent introduction of the Reddito di Cittadinanza has strongly reinforced conditionalities. The payment of the benefit is conditional on the immediate employment availability of the family members over 18 years old, excluding the Citizenship Pension beneficiaries, the disabled, the members with family responsibility for minors under three years of age or family members with serious disabilities, and those who are already attending a training course or are employed in low-wage jobs (with incomes below 8,000 euros, 4,800 for self-employed workers). The new minimum income distinguishes between beneficiaries who are exempt from job-search conditionalities and beneficiaries subject to a 'work-pact' who are required to accept one of three 'suitable' job offers within the first 18 months of receiving the payment. A job offer is considered reasonable depending on the wage level and the distance from the beneficiary's residence. On the other hand, the RdC is immediately suspended if one of the family members does not give immediate availability to work, does not sign the 'Patto per il lavoro' (work placement agreement) or the 'Patto per l'inclusione sociale' (social inclusion pact), does not participate in training programmes, does not accept at least one among the three suitable job offers.[1] In addition to work-conditionalities recipients are required to make themselves available for eight hours a week (up to a maximum of 16 hours) for community-work activities provided by local authorities.

The comparison with France and Germany is particularly interesting here. After years of substantial immobility, Italy has started to overcome the delay it had accumulated within a short period of time. However, the new system's structure is ambiguous. On the one hand, the Reddito di Cittadinanza represents an unprecedented increase in public expenditure. On the other hand, it reinforces the workfarist and disciplinary approach, close to that of the Hartz reforms in Germany, with the additional constraint of unpaid work (up to a maximum of 16 hours per week) in community work as a condition for accessing the benefit. Second, unlike other reforms we have analysed – both Hartz IV and Prime Activité – the Reddito di Cittadinanza does not provide for any tax credit or cumulation mechanism with a low-paid job. In many European countries, this mechanism implies that only a share of the income is taken into account for the access requirements, thus making it more convenient for the beneficiary to combine labour income and minimum income support and, on the other hand, discouraging welfare dependency. With the new centre-right government taking office at the end of 2022, a major revision of the Citizenship Income is underway. As of 2024, the Italian minimum income is supposed to split into two different instruments, one welfare aimed at the non-employable poor, the other for employable beneficiaries. For the latter, the subsidy will be significantly reduced through a work-first tightening of labour insertion measures.

3.4 Minimum income and community work

Involvement in community work or community service in order to subsidies is in force in several countries. In Denmark, all recipients are required to participate in an activation programme that varies according to the person's level of employability (Kvist 2015). If they do not find a job within the first three months, they are required to participate in community work in exchange for the minimum income. As mentioned earlier, the reforms implemented between 2014 and 2016 are characterised, on the one hand, by the reduction of benefits for certain social groups (young people and residents for less than 7 years) and, on the other, by the introduction of a workfare logic that links the eligibility for the full minimum income to the work performance, whether in the framework of the subsidy (community work) or not.

Participation in community work is also a requirement for those considered unemployable in the ordinary labour market. People who are considered unable to work in community work due to serious social problems are nevertheless obliged to participate in a resource programme that commits them to access other services, for example, care.

In Germany, after the Hartz reforms, Jobcentres have had several specific employment insertion programmes available for those who are most difficult to relocate. Among these, it is worth mentioning the so-called Ein-Euro-Jobs, introduced in 2005 within the framework of the Hartz reforms, targeting some minimum income recipients. The aim of the programme is to provide opportunities for employment in the public or non-profit sectors in jobs that are not in competition with the employees of the involved organisations. This requirement is designed to prevent possible dumping effects and, more generally, the downward spiral of salaries in the primary sector by non-market subsidised jobs. In addition to this, the participant receives a monthly payment to cover the work carried out, consisting of one euro per hour worked to be associated with the minimum income, hence the term Ein-Euro-Jobs. Alongside this programme, there are also other instruments to promote access to employment, such as the Kommunal-Kombi, launched in 2008 with a mix of national and European funds and aimed at supporting the employment, for a maximum of three years, of the most disadvantaged people in community work in non-profit organisations and local authorities in areas of high unemployment (79 in total, of which 71 are located in the eastern Lander). According to Wolff and Stephan (2013), between 2005 and 2010, the number of beneficiaries rose from 603,000 to 343,000, with a peak of 796,000 in 2006. Meanwhile, the allocated expenditure more than halved between 2005 and 2012: from €895 million to €358 million (ibid). However, it remains a relevant tool for facilitating the entry into the labour market of the most at-risk target groups, including asylum seekers.

But beyond the numbers, a no less important aspect concerns the quality of the created employment. Several analyses highlight how the quantitative growth of work has not been matched by an equal improvement in working conditions (Hohmeyer and Wolff 2012), actually relegating many of the beneficiaries to a sort of secondary labour market, not too different from the subsidised work circuits that were at the centre of the experience of community work in many European countries, including Italy and France itself with the Insertion programmes. These programmes, especially the RMI (Revenue Minimum Insertion), were often placed somewhere between subsidised work, training and dedicated social security, with the explicit objective of directly creating work for unemployed people in personal care or community work. In France, these policies have certainly contributed to the growth of regular employment as well as to the emergence of undeclared work (see Ciarini's Chapter 4). The problem is that they have been much less effective in qualifying the work of those involved as recipients of insertion plans. According to Dares (2018), more than 20% of Minima Sociaux recipients are employed in these sectors (compared to an average of 8% for other sectors). In contrast, there is no requirement to be involved in free activities in order to receive a subsidy. In 2017, such a case was approved at the departmental level (Haut-Rhin), under the name of RSA-bénévolat. After a dispute between the prefecture (representing the government) and the departmental council, the State Council authorised this measure in 2018, but limited it to seven hours per week. However, it remains a minority area and has nothing to do with some recent measures aimed at financially recognising – for all citizens, however, not just some disadvantaged groups – engagement in off-market activities, such as the 'compte d'engagement citoyen'. These issues will be further discussed in Chapter 6. Here it is worth emphasising that in comparison with these different experiences of off-market activation, Italian legislation opens up a significant extension of free work to community work as a requirement for receiving a subsidy for all. It is not part of the activation programmes dedicated to the most marginal groups or those who are difficult to relocate, as is the case in Denmark and Germany. All beneficiaries subject to obligations are bound by this condition. The reform that introduced the Reddito di Cittadinanza states that community projects are owned by the municipalities and can be carried out in cooperation with not-for-profit organisations in some specific areas: culture, social affairs, environment, training, and the common good. But those in receipt of benefits cannot be used to replace (even temporarily) the employees of public administrations or external service providers. Despite these constraints, it is nonetheless a rule that links the use of a subsidy to off-market work activity for several hours per week that has been increased to 16 from the 8 hours initially foreseen.

3.5 Conclusions

Even though there are different time frames and intervention strategies that are not always comparable, minimum income policies, and, more generally, policies for fighting poverty, have become part of the European welfare systems not only as last resort networks but also as ways of supplementing the income of the working poor. Alongside these instruments, tax measures such as tax deductions and tax credits to increase net income received, and the range of social services and benefits that supplement the costs of childcare, health and housing have also started to become more important. They have, over time, become a significant part of anti-poverty measures. However, this trend towards the taxation of counteracting poorly paid work, as Sara Marchal and Ive Marx (2018) defined it, does not concern all beneficiaries. There are additional interventions that tend to target certain groups of beneficiaries who are more at risk, both of being caught in poverty and of being dependent on benefits, such as single mothers, single-parent families, and those with minor children, especially those with low employment intensity. All this, while it widens the intervention scope available to policy makers, makes intervention management more complex, leaving other groups of beneficiaries less at risk but no less affected by the problem of poor work. This shift affects not only existing work towards which the beneficiaries of the benefits are oriented but also that which is created by means of the various instruments designed to increase job placement. There are problems here that are worth focusing on. While conditionality, active labour market policies, and the various tax credits can play a positive role in mitigating passive dependence on benefits, especially for those most at risk, this is not enough to guarantee labour insertion, or qualify the work that is generated. In addition, academic research tells us that making benefits conditional on work, pushes people to accept any job or to work in conditions that do not equate to those of regular workers in the labour market (Girardi et al. 2019).

From this point of view, although significant differences remain between the countries considered here in terms of the generosity and extent of benefits, what we find is a general trend towards strengthening sanctions and punitive work conditionalities. Compared to other approaches, focusing on investment in training and the achievement of social and labour inclusion, the intervention methods that tend to be deployed shift the problem of combating poverty from the absence of income to the absence of employment. However, this results in accentuating precarity (Pulignano 2018). The case of Denmark is representative. It remains, in terms of expenditure and generosity of benefits, one of the countries with the highest redistributive impact, even if it has declined over the years. However, reforms have gone forward with increasingly more emphasis on work-first and with ever greater responsibility being placed on individuals for being unemployed.

The same can be said for those countries that have significantly increased their spending and the number of beneficiaries, such as Italy. While there has been an unprecedented increase in resources to fight poverty, the system dedicated to labour reintegration is characterised by a more pronounced workfarist orientation. Moreover, it includes activation strategies that go beyond the boundaries of paid market work, by including non-market, unpaid work in community services. As for France and Germany, here we are faced with policy systems that have raised the bar of conditionality but to difference levels. In France, the fight against poverty remains more generous in terms of resources than in countries like Germany. It is less subject to conditionality, but it is also relatively more expensive, with all the consequences of pressure on social spending and a very high proportion of people dependent on the various Minima Sociaux. In contrast, in Germany, the Hartz IV reforms have contributed to increasing active labour market participation and keeping social expenditure under control, but at the cost of a sharp increase in the risk of poverty among the employed and also among benefit recipients, as can be seen in Figures 3.3 and 3.4.

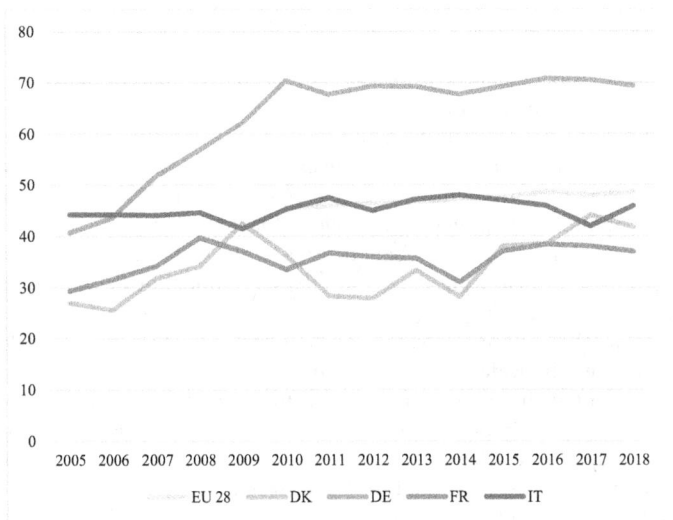

Figure 3.3 People at risk of poverty, unemployed, % Years 2008–2018
Source: Author's elaboration from the Eurostat online database

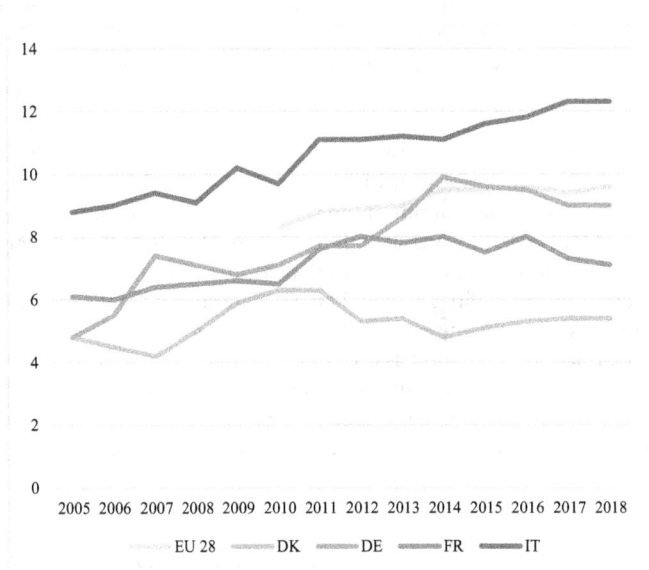

Figure 3.4 People at risk of poverty, temporary workers, % Years 2008–2018
Source: Author's elaboration from the Eurostat online database

Based on our analysis, we can make the following remarks. First, many of these measures have seen a shift to work-first over the years – in some cases, like Germany, even before the crisis. However, this does not relieve them from the problem of the working poor. Secondly, even if work incentives mitigate a passive reliance on welfare, they do not contribute per se to improving the quality of the work that is created in the labour market, as shown by the experience of the mini-jobs, and, though in France this is limited to the care sector, by the French method of integrating social policies and policies for directly creating personal services for Minima Sociaux beneficiaries. Finally, the hybridisation of low-paid and unpaid work enters into the conditionalities linked to the receipt of benefits. These interlinks reflect different forms of market and off-market activation, which combine with social policies in order to guarantee the widest possible labour insertion. The outcome is that employment includes non-market activities, but the 'deserving poor' have to accept this work in order to access their subsidy; otherwise, the subsidy will be suspended. In some countries, it remains a minority measure, that is, dedicated to the most marginalised sectors of the population, and in Germany and Denmark, it is little used. It is illegal in France, where labour insertion and conditionality remain linked to market activation, not off-market activities. By contrast, in Italy – the country that has implemented this measure later compared to others, but who had a very significant increase in expenditure – this requirement applies to all minimum income recipients.

Due to the pressure to reduce public expenditure, minimum income schemes have undergone several changes. Compared to an initial phase in which these instruments were essentially conceived as passive measures to alleviate poverty, over the years they undergone a work-first torsion to strengthen the incentive to work, even at the price of low-income and precarious jobs at the margins of the labour market. In parallel, the beneficiaries have been growing steadily, including working poor and beneficiaries cumulating a subsidy and a low-paid jobs. Together with stricter job-search conditionalities in-work benefits became part of the minimum income support. In many cases, however, this broadening of instruments to support labour insertion has not contributed to a real improvement in anti-poverty policies. Rather than contribute to cushioning economic and social shocks, these types of minimum incomes legitimise the creation of low-paid, though subsidise, jobs at the margins of the labour market.

Note

1   In addition to the above-mentioned cases, disqualification from the RdC also occurs when the beneficiary fails to communicate a change of employment status or provides false information or is found to be carrying out other work

without having declared it. Whoever submits false declarations or documents is punished with detention for two to six years. Moreover, if the person neglects to communicate changes in income, assets, or other relevant information for the purpose of benefit revocation or reduction, the penalty is one to three years' detention.

References

Alber, J., Heisig, J.P. (2011) *Do New Labour Activation Policies work? A Descriptive Analysis of the German Hartz Reforms.* WZB Discussion Paper n. SP I 2011-211, Wissenschaftszentrum Berlin für Sozialforschung (WZB), Berlin, September.

Baccaro, L., Benassi, C. (2014) Softening industrial relations institutions, hardening growth model: The transformation of the German political economy. *Stato e Mercato*, 3, pp. 369–395.

Barbieri, P., Cutuli, G., Scherer, S. (2018) In-work poverty in un mercato del lavoro duale: individualizzazione riflessiva dei rischi sociali o stratificazione della diseguaglianza sociale? *Stato e Mercato*, 3, pp. 419–460.

Cantillon, B., Parolin, Z., Collado, D. (2020) A glass ceiling on poverty reduction? An empirical investigation into the structural constraints on minimum income protections. *Journal of European Social Policy*, 30(2), pp. 129–143.

Ciarini, A. (2016) Policies to boost services and employment in the long-term care sector. A downward convergence towards low-wage service jobs in the European Welfare State? *Stato e Mercato*, 1, pp. 119–151.

Ciarini, A., Rizza, R. (2021) How stable is dualisation? The case of labour market and antipoverty policies in Italy. *Sociologia del lavoro*, 159, pp. 89–110.

Collado, D., Cantillon, B., Van den Bosch, K., Goedemé, T., Vandelannoote, D. (2016) *The End of Cheap Talk about Poverty Reduction: The Cost of Closing the Poverty Gap While Maintaining Work Incentives* (Improve Working Paper no. 16/08). Antwerp: Herman Deleeck Centre for Social Policy, University of Antwerp.

Dares. (2018a) *Les salariés des services à la personne: comment évoluent leurs conditions de travail et d'emploi?* Paris: Dares Analyses.

Diop-Christensen, A. (2018) Beating the "unemployable" with a stick: The effect of economic incentives on unemployed immigrants and their social welfare workers. In: Kamala, M., Jönsson, J.H. (eds) *Neoliberalism, Nordic Welfare States and Social Work: Current and Future Challenges*. London: Routledge, pp. 205–215.

Drees. (2017) *Minima sociaux et prestations sociales – Ménages aux revenus modestes et redistribution*. Paris: Edition 2017.

Drees. (2021) *Minima sociaux et prestations sociales. Ménages aux revenus modestes et redistribution*. Paris: Edition 2018.

Eichhorst, W., Hassel, A. (2018) The German exception: Welfare protectionism instead of retrenchment. In: Theodoropoulou, S. (eds) *Labour Market Policies in the Era of Pervasive Austerity: A European Perspective*. Bristol: Bristol University Press, pp. 115–140.

Eichhorst, W., Marx, P. (2012) Whatever works: Dualisation and the service economy in Bismarckian welfare states. In: Emmenegger, P., Häusermann, S., Palier, B., Seeleib-Kaise, M. (eds) *The Age of Dualization: The Changing Face of Inequality in Deindustrializing Societies*. Oxford: Oxford University Press, pp. 73–99.

Eichhorst, W., Marx, P. (2009) *Reforming German Labor Market Institutions: A Dual Path to Flexibility.* IZA Discussion Paper, Bonn. 4100, March.

Emin. (2015) Toward adequate and accessible Minimum Income Schemes in Europe. Analysis of Minimum Income Schemes and roadmaps in 30 countries participating in the EMIN project, Synthesis report, European Union, Bruxelles.

Girardi, S., Pulignano, V., Maas, R. (2019), Activated and included? The social inclusion of social assistance beneficiaries engaged in "public works". *International Journal of Sociology and Social Policy,* 39(9/10), pp. 738–751.

Hansen, M. (2019) *The Moral Economy of Activation: Ideas, Politics and Policies.* Bristol: Policy Press.

Hohmeyer, K., Wolff, J. (2012) A fistful of euros: Is the German one-euro job workfare scheme effective for participants? *International Journal of Social Welfare,* 21, pp. 174–185.

Immervoll, H., Pearson, M. (2009) *A Good Time for Making Work Pay? Taking Stock of In-Work Benefits and Related Measures across the OECD* (OECD Social, Employment and Migration Working Papers n. 81). Paris: OECD.

INPS. (2020) *XIX Rapporto annuale INPS.* Roma: INPS.

INPS. (2022) *XXI Rapporto annuale INPS.* Roma: INPS.

ISTAT. (2020) *Nel 2019 in calo la povertà assoluta* (Rapporto. 16 giugno 2020). Roma: Rapporto.

Kvist, J. (2015) *ESPN Thematic Report on Minimum Income Schemes in Denmark.* Brussels: European Social Policy Network.

Larsen, P.K. (2017) *EMIN Context Report Denmark. Developments in Relation to Minimum Income Schemes.* Copenhagen: European Minimum Income Network Denmark.

Lodemel, I., Trickey, H. (eds) (2001) *An Offer You Can't Refuse: Workfare in International Perspective.* Bristol: Policy Press.

Marchal, S., Marx, I. (2018) Stemming the tide: What have EU countries done to support low-wage workers in an era of downward wage pressures? *Journal of European Social Policy,* 28(1), pp. 18–33.

Marchal, S., Van Mechelen, N. (2017) A new kid in town? Active inclusion elements in European minimum income schemes. *Social Policy & Administration,* 51(1), pp. 171–194.

Murray, C. (1990) *The Emerging British Underclass.* London: Institute of Economic Affairs.

Natili, M. (2017) Reddito minimo nel Sud Europa. Quali sviluppi con la Grande Recessione? *La Rivista della Politiche Sociali,* 3, pp. 119–133.

Natili, M. (2018) *The Politics of Minimum Income. Explaining Path Departure and Policy Reversal in the Age of Austerity.* Hoboken: Palgrave Macmillan.

Pulignano, V. (2018) Precarious work, regime of competition and the case of Europe. In: Kalleberg, A.L., Vallas, S.P. (eds) *Precarious Work.* Bingley: Emerald Publishing, pp. 33–60.

Sacchi, S., Gallo, G. (2019) *Beneficiari e spesa del reddito di cittadinanza: una stima della misura finale* (Policy Brief, n. 11). Roma: INAPP.

Saraceno, C., Benassi, D., Morlicchio, E. (2020) *Poverty in Italy Features and Drivers in a European Perspective.* Bristol: Policy Press.

Schmid, G. (2018) *Inclusive Growth: The Case of Germany.* IZA Policy Paper n. 139, June.

Vesan, P., Pavolini, E. (2018) The Italian labour market policy reforms and the economic crisis: coming towards the end of Italian exceptionalism? In: Theodoropoulou, S. (eds) *Labour Market Policies in the Era of Pervasive Austerity: A European Perspective.* Bristol: Policy Press, pp. 69–90.

Vlandas, T. (2013) The politics of temporary work deregulation in Europe: Solving the French puzzle. *Politics & Society,* 41(3), pp. 425–460.

Wolff, J., Stephan, G. (2013) Subsidized work before and after the German Hartz reforms: Design of major schemes, evaluation results and lessons learnt. *IZA Journal of Labor Policy,* 2, 16.

4 Social policies and employment in personal care services

The working poor and services in times of austerity

Andrea Ciarini

4.1 Introduction

Social investment policies have a double nature. On the one hand, they embrace a productive vision of welfare through investments in services, education, and human capital, aimed at increasing employability and supporting a high path to competitiveness (Bonoli and Natali 2012; Hemerijck 2012; see also Crouch in this volume). On the other hand, Social Investment (SI) responds to the need to tackle the new social risks. As may authors emphasised (Esping-Andersen et al. 2002; Bonoli 2005; Hemerijck 2012, 2013) poverty, family needs, and work-life balance, as well as to elderly care and long-term care are at the centre of the new welfare supply towards new social risks. For all countries, the strengthening of in-kind provision is a necessary condition to better respond to more complex social needs and relieve the family from care tasks that would otherwise negatively affect women in particular. This trend also reflects a growing labour demand related to service provision, both at home and in residential settings. For several years now, employment in social services has been growing steadily. As can be seen from Table 4.1, welfare services are among the sectors that have contributed most to creating new jobs, even in the years of the crisis. The data at the European level (EU 28 average) are significant in this regard. Compared to a loss of around three million jobs between 2008 and 2018 in manufacturing (–7.8%) and 3.1 (–17%) in construction and the essentially stable trend of employment in public administration (–0.8%), social services, residential, and home care, recorded an increase of 2.3 million new employees (+37.6% in residential care; +19.9% in home care).

This process is transversal to most European countries, although with some specific features. Sweden and Denmark are two countries characterised, by high levels of employment in welfare (in line with the tradition of the Nordic systems; see Figure 4.1). Except for Sweden, in so far as residential services are concerned, and Denmark, as far as home care

DOI: 10.4324/9781003369707-4

Table 4.1 The variation of employment in some European countries by productive sector (Nace Rev. 2), Val. %, Years 2008–2018

	Eu28	Germany	France	Italy	Spain	Denmark	Sweden	United Kingdom
Manufacturing	−7.8	−2.1	−15.2	−7.6	−18.2	−23.6	−19.2	−15.0
Building	−17	8.6	−6.5	−28.6	−50.5	−12.2	14.4	−12.7
Public administration	−0.8	3.8	−8.8	−14.4	3.3	−17.6	37.6	−0.6
Residential care services	37.6	37.9	41.6	36.3	38.1	4.7	−6.0	118.7
Residential care services	19.9	41.6	30.1	27.9	40.2	−3.3	23.4	−8.4

Source: Author's elaboration from the Eurostat online database – Labour Force Survey

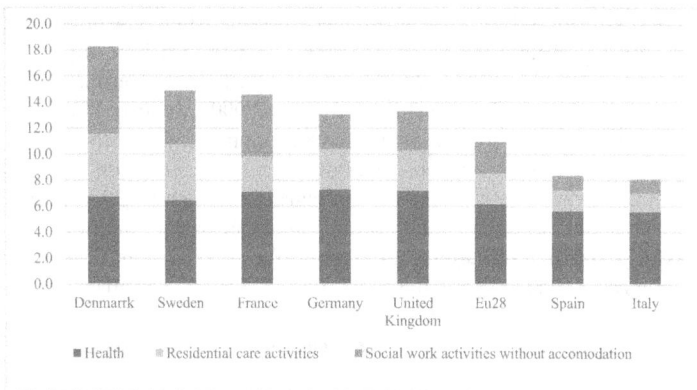

Figure 4.1 The employment composition in health and social services (residential and home care), Val. percentage of total employment, Year 2018

Source: Our elaboration on Eurostat data – Labour Force Survey

services are concerned, all the main European countries show positive percentage deviations. The overall share of this employment remains different, with striking differences between the various country clusters. First, we should consider the weight of the family in the delivery of services. In Mediterranean countries, many of these services are traditionally entrusted to the family, while in Anglo-Saxon countries they are entrusted to the market and in Scandinavian countries to direct public provision. More generally, we should also consider the employment distribution between health care and social services. In the health sector, employment may be regulated by the National Health Service, as in Italy, the United Kingdom and Sweden, or through the compulsory social insurance system, as in France and Germany. In this context, if employment in health services is not lower in Italy than in most of the countries under consideration, the same cannot be said of the social and care sector, which is, in fact, understaffed, especially with respect to the large share of informal and irregular work within households.

Another element to take into account concerns the welfare mix between public, private, and services provided by not-for-profit organisations. To summarise, we can distinguish between (Meagher and Sze-behely 2013; Favarque 2013; Carbonnier and Morel 2015):

- contexts with a traditional public vocation but strong growth of the private market (large: multinational service companies operating under an agreement with the public or directly paid for by users): Sweden, Denmark;
- contexts with a traditional subsidiary vocation, where the non-profit sector is prevalent but where there is a growth of private supply by smaller enterprises and individual workers: France, Germany, Belgium (and after the reforms of the mid-2000s, Spain). These are countries that, in recent years, have implemented reforms aimed at providing users with vouchers and tax relief, enabling them to purchase care in a regulated social market in which both individual professionals and private and non-profit organisations operate;
- contexts with a market vocation, where both public and non-profit offers are weak: United Kingdom and Anglo-Saxon countries. These are countries that have substantially privatised welfare services, transferring most of the social services from the public sector to the market;
- contexts with a subsidiary vocation but with a large undeclared work component that existing policies continue to feed, negatively affecting the emergence of a regular personal services market: Italy, Greece. In these countries, a declining public sector is counterbalanced by a non-profit sector traditionally involved in some services and a large component of undeclared work (black market) reflecting the lack of a coherent policy framework. The black market issue is not specific to this group of countries. However, it is precisely in this group that the phenomenon is most severe.

The main problem that many European countries are facing is that this growth in employment is influenced by low-wage and low-qualified jobs. In many cases, this trend was a consequence of reforms that intentionally contributed to lowering the cost of labour so as to raise the in-kind provision in the private sector (Colombo et al. 2011; Eichhorst and Marx 2012; Favarque 2013; Ciarini 2016). Whilst this problem is affected by the labour-intensive nature of these services – with all that this implies in terms of lower labour productivity – and also by the high percentage of female employment – which is more subject to the gender pay gap – there is a trade-off between employment growth and low wages that budgetary constraints tend to enhance. As shown by many authors (Iversen and Wren 1998; Esping-Andersen 2000; Carbonnier and Morel 2015), this trade-off is related to Baumol's so-called 'cost disease', that is, the fact that in labour-intensive services (including social work), there is structurally low labour productivity, which means low wage pressure under market conditions. In personal social services, this low productivity is linked to the relational nature of the services provided. This is a constraint that can only be solved either through the provision of public services – and therefore public employment – or through high levels of social spending to cover the productivity gaps that private solutions, both profit and not-for-profit, tend to offload on labour costs (Iversen and Wren 1998; Esping-Andersen 2000).

Breaking out of this cycle implies more social spending. But it is precisely at this point that the key issue arises. How can employment in personal and social services be developed, whether in the field of care for the elderly, childcare, health protection, or work-life balance, given their structurally low unit productivity or the rising costs that some types of services require? Given the budgetary constraints that not only prevent an increase in social spending but also exert downward pressure triggered by the austerity measures, new solutions have emerged to reduce the cost of labour as the only way to favour the expansion of in-kind supply.

The presence of these trade-offs is common in several European countries. There is, of course, an alternative: governments can choose to increase employment in services through public spending, as in the Scandinavian countries, but at the cost of an increased tax burden. In fact, this option has been under pressure in these northern countries. Countries such as Sweden, but also Denmark, traditionally characterised by high rates of public employment in social services have introduced tax relief for domestic work and some personal services, alongside reforms that opened to a market service provision (Meagher and Szebehely 2013).

Remarkably, at the European level, the Commission (2012, 2018) has also encouraged the adoption of tax reductions and deductions, with vouchers, in order to reduce labour costs and foster job creation within families. Some studies (Favarque 2013) have shown that the introduction of these policy tools has helped in reducing the amount of undeclared work, supporting the creation of new regular (low-paid) jobs for a wide range of personal services, especially in households. In addition, there are concerns regarding the distributive effects of these reforms. As

Devetter and Lefebvre (2015) have pointed out in relation to France – the country that has invested most in this social and employment policy – while vouchers and tax relief have contributed to reducing the incidence of undeclared work within households, they have also had a negative impact on wages and the skill level of social workers at home. Finally, Devetter and Lefebvre (ibid.) point out the presence of a form of adverse selection that mainly rewards, among the final recipients of the reductions, the population groups with higher incomes. These are in fact those who have benefited most from this policy of encouraging the purchase of services at low labour costs.

For Italy, the issue is even more complex, because it is more influenced not only by the family balance inherited from the past and by a low expenditure on social services but also by the absence in recent years of a coherent strategy for personal and social services. In spite of reforms aimed at promoting regular employment, it is rather the informal economy that has driven the development of personal and social services at home, with even worse consequences than in other countries, given the large pool of irregular work that persists in the care system. In the following sections, we will examine the institutional entanglements behind these different reform strategies with reference to some particularly significant national cases: Italy, France, and Germany.

4.2   Social and employment policies to create jobs in social services: comparing France and Germany

4.2.1 *Social policy reforms and social work*

Transformations in welfare systems affect not only the nature and extent of social benefits but also the care labour market, whether formal or informal. This link is particularly significant in the countries we have chosen to analyse, especially France and Germany. As many authors have pointed out (Eichhorst and Marx 2012) it is also through social policy reforms that these two countries have stimulated the creation of new employment at the labour market edge. They have overcome former inflexibility that, in the previous model of so-called 'jobless welfare' (Esping-Andersen 2002; Pierson 2001; Eichhorst and Marx 2012), contributed to reducing the volume of formal employment in personal services. According to that model, a strong and stable core of guaranteed high-productivity (male) employment, in industrial sectors, was compensated for by a low level of unpaid female care work in the home. In many ways, from the persistent rigidity of standard employment to the lesser development of low-productivity tertiary employment to the comparatively large share of the unemployed (young people and women above all) on welfare, this model has stood alone for some time.

It could not be defined either by the changing trajectories of the Anglo-Saxon countries, which started to develop services earlier through market-based private employment, or by the Scandinavian countries, where state employment has historically supported the expansion of welfare services.

Since the second half of the 2000s, several social and labour reforms have contributed to changing this model. The changes aimed to foster, firstly, the creation of new jobs, albeit ones paying low wages and the outsourcing of services previously linked to the family. The second aim was to keep social spending under control, subject to more budgetary constraints than in the past.

However, there are some differences between these two countries in terms of the type of strategy they have adopted. For example, according to the classification once suggested by Da Roit and Weicht (2013) France and Germany adopted two distinct employment models of care. The first, the German one, focused on a combination of formal and informal family work, supported by social policies, while the second, the French one, was aimed more at promoting formal employment.

The reforms introduced in France at once favoured the development of the social services market based on demand solvency instruments, extensively financed by the public, with widely used vouchers. From the same perspective, the service social market was then reorganised in 2005 around a single instrument, the Cheque Emploi Service Universel (CESU), which allowed households to access a wide range of services, from small repair and home-work services, childcare, to highly integrated social and health services, including the comprehensive non-self-sufficiency support system.

Until the first half of the 2000s, the French personal services sector was characterised by strong supply segmentation. With a very small number of enterprises operating in the sector, most employment relationships directly involved the client and the individual worker, often in the undeclared work sector, creating a very similar context to that still prevailing in Italy today. With an integrated strategy of reforms able to jointly act on tax and social security benefits for the regularisation of labour relations and on the revision of welfare provisions – first with the institution of the APA (Allocation Personalisée d'Autonomie) in 2002, then with the CESU in 2005, which extended the use of the universal voucher to all personal care services – the premises for strong growth in regular employment have been created in a few years, with positive effects also for the State in terms of tax revenues and financial contributions, and also for the establishment of profit and non-profit enterprises.

These policies have facilitated the emergence of many social care services delivered at home in the informal market, contributing to the development of regular employment in personal care. They have also provided a tool for the occupational inclusion of groups most at the edge of the labour market, unemployed or long-term unemployed, under the welfare schemes against poverty – first the Revenue Minimum Insertion, since 2009 the Revenue Solidarité Active. More on this in the following paragraph.

The system of personal services in France is today based on a single solvency instrument, the CESU, divided into two main procedures for benefit management and delivery: the CESU déclaratif and the CESU préfinancé. The CESU déclaratif is a voucher directly used by employers to purchase a range of services at home: household services, repair work, babysitting, school support, administrative assistance, care for the elderly and non-self-sufficient people, home security tasks, and preparing meals.

The relationship between the contractors involves an employment contract for remuneration that cannot be lower than the SMIC minimum wage. What is of benefit are the high contribution allowances guaranteed by the State, which in fact reduce the gross cost to the employer, to the point of making it inconvenient to hire 'off the books'. The CESU préfinancé, on the other hand, is a voucher whose amount is financed exante by an employer, public or private, as part of the supplementary benefits provided for employees (CESU Ressources humaines) or by a public, social, or welfare body, in order to provide a series of care and social or sociomedical assistance services at home (CESU Social). The APA follows this second approach; it was introduced in 2002, and since 2005, it has been integrated into the system of personal services regulated by CESU. From an operational point of view, voucher allocation is linked to the evaluation of the case by a medical-social team at the departmental level (in Italy, corresponding to the provinces), with the task of assessing the user's state of need, through an evaluation grid arranged into four levels. Based on this, the voucher provision anticipates a wide range of options to which the user can have access, whether residential or home-based, provided by an individual provider hired directly by the beneficiary, by a family member (other than the spouse), by an accredited third sector association, by a private company, or by the authorities (Colombo et al. 2011; Angermann and Eichhorst 2012).

In contrast, in Germany, the social market for services has, at least until recent years, been based on a different combination of formal and informal-family care. This combination was fostered by the first reforms that put the social security system in order, starting with the introduction of the new social insurance for non-self-sufficiency in 1994. These differences in the share of formal and informal work reflect, first of all, a different legislative focus on supporting family caregiving, which has typically been more compliant in Germany than in France (Ciarini

2016). For example, pension coverage for family caregivers was provided in the case of social insurance for non-self-sufficiency (Pflegeversicherung) (Rothgang 2011). This was not the case in France, where formal recognition of family caregiving was limited to the potential transfer of part of the amount received to a family member other than a spouse or partner. Moreover, no social security coverage was provided for the family caregiver. Conversely, in Germany, the monitoring of the actual use of the amounts is much less strict. This aspect has been crucial, according to many (Bettio and Mazzotta 2011; Colombo et al. 2011; Simonazzi and Picchi 2013), in favouring, at least initially, family work and a large pool of the illegal workforce, mostly immigrants (Colombo et al. 2011; Bode and Chartrand 2011). In addition, many of the care regime studies referred to above had already highlighted the differences between Germany, which is more anchored in the tradition of the male breadwinner family, and France, which seemed to be moving towards greater support for formal services.

However, recent trends in how transfers are used in Germany show a decrease in the monetary solution tout court for family caregivers and an increase in home and residential services (Rothgang 2011), both in terms of users and number of workers involved, reflecting a gradual shift towards private profit and non-profit providers.

These changes show that the care work market is being formalised, as attested to by the increase of private, profit, and non-profit providers (Bode and Chartrand 2011). For instance, if in the most recent years, for-profit providers have come to cover about half of the residential market in long-term care, their share of more than 60% of the home-based services market is even higher (Ciarini 2016). In contrast, public supply is residual. In addition to the increasing share of employment within for-profit and not-for-profit providers, there is also an increase in employment within households as a consequence of the reforms that introduced mini-jobs (Simonazzi and Picchi 2013; Favarque 2013). But this will be discussed in the next section.

4.2.2 The impact on the labour market and working conditions

With regard to the employment patterns linked to vouchers, there are three different types of employment relationships in France: direct employment, so called 'gré à gré', by which a worker is employed by the user to carry out activities at home, 'mandataire' employment: through an accredited intermediary agency for the provision of home-based labour; and finally, the possible 'prestataire' organisations, that is, accredited service providers, mostly private. These different solutions, especially in-home care, are not in conflict with each other, but the beneficiary can use different delivery options at the same time, combining different services in the social care market.

From a job creation policy perspective, one of the main advantages of this model has been the strong impulse to coordinate the different services that comprise personal care (Simonazzi and Picchi 2013), from mild interventions such as help with household tasks to more complex services at a higher social and health integration level. Thanks to this wide range of vouchers and tax credits, the personal care sector has been developing rapidly in terms of employment. In 2010, the number of people employed was 1.5 million, 74% of whom were employed directly by the household, and the remaining 26% by an organisation outside the household. More recent data indicate a contraction in the number of people involved: in 2016, 1.22 million, roughly corresponding to 500 thousand full-time employed (Dares 2018b). This is a decrease that, however, is also affected by the economic recession. Moreover, compared to 2004, before the reorganisation of the personal services sector, there has been a 70% increase in the number of regular employees (Drees 2014). There is no doubt that in quantitative terms, the integration into a single instrument (the CESU) of the different access and purchase channels of in-home personal care services has made a positive contribution to the creation of new regular employment, which, however, remains low-paid and labour-intensive: an average of 887 hours per year compared to an average of 1,404 among employees (Dares 2018a). On the other hand, according to several authors (Guiraudon and Ledoux 2015; Carbonnier and Morel 2015), integrating domestic services and more structured welfare services into a single instrument, up to and including highly integrated social and health services, has resulted in a deterioration in the quality of the latter, especially in terms of job qualification and recognition of social work.

Furthermore, it must be said that the State supported the costs of these work incentive policies. The mere objective of discouraging the undeclared market requires an intervention to reduce the gross by at least the difference from net costs. Tax exemption and VAT tax relief cost 3.8 billion euros per year. Also, 3.5 billion are allocated to tax credits. If we add to this the approximately 4.4 billion for direct aid, that is, social expenditure for dependent and long-term care, we reach a total value of about 11.7 billion (Cour des Compte 2014; Lebrun 2015). This is a huge cost. However, according to the advocates for this policy, it has the capacity to nourish a regular market for personal care services that guarantees resources and tax revenues for the government. It has been estimated that out of 11 billion in outlays for the state, there are nine billion in revenues for a final cost of two billion (Lebrun 2015). In contrast, others argue that even by doing so, the cost to the state not only is high but mainly favours higher-income groups who can benefit most from the incentives, without any particular qualification of the work that is actually generated (Devetter and Lefebvre 2015).

In Germany, the policy of tax relief and incentives to create regular employment is due in large part to the Hartz reforms and the introduction of mini-jobs. A difference with France emerges here. While in France this kind of instrument was expressly dedicated to employment in care and domestic work (through CESU), in Germany the spread of mini-jobs covered the whole spectrum of low-productivity tertiary sectors: trade, catering, and care. From this point of view, they are similar in their basic approach to Italian 'accessory work', which is also regulated by vouchers that can be used in a wide range of sectors, at least until its abolition in 2017 (more on this in the following paragraph). As has already been shown earlier (see Chapter 3 y Ciarini, Girardi, and Pulignano), the growth of mini-jobs, which employ mainly women and account for 7.6 million according to recent data reported by Schmid (2018), has run parallel to the decrease in unemployment but also to the increase in the risk of poverty linked to work. In total, there are 300 thousand mini-jobs in home-based personal care services (ibid). But salaried employment in social services is also on the rise, along with the increasing use of outsourcing in the social services market. However, even here, the work that is created is subject to low wages. Several factors affect this issue, first and foremost the relational nature of services, which in fact underlies lower labour productivity and consequently lower wages on the market. However, there are also very specific policy decisions to contain labour costs and thus contribute to the expansion of formal benefits in the presence of monitored social expenditure. In this respect, it is worth recalling that with the introduction of social insurance for non-self-sufficiency it was decided to fix wage levels at 10% below those of the public sector (ibid). It was not until 2010 that a minimum hourly wage for care workers was introduced. In general terms, apart from a small group of professional care workers, mostly employed in residential care and more socially integrated services, who have experienced wage increases in recent years, the vast majority of care workers have suffered from worsening contractual conditions, through low wages, reductions in hours, and the increasing use of temporary workers (see Eichhorst et al. 2013). According to data reported by Eichhorst, Marx, and Tobsch (ivi) the use of part-time work in the care sector is 50%. In addition to this, according to estimates of the trade union Verdi, reported by Simonazzi and Picchi (2013), 72% of these workers are at wage levels that qualify for the guaranteed minimum income (Arbeitslosengeld II). This is important because it is part, albeit indirectly, of this strategy of low-wage employment growth in services. If we consider the large number of workers in the personal care sector accessing minimum income benefits, we can see how this connection is an essential part of the trade-off between the expansion of social services and low wages. The combinations and intensities of

these connections are different. Also in France, the number of beneficiaries of minimum income measures who are employed in personal
services is high, a quarter of the total according to the most recent data
(Drees 2019). Counting only employees, the share of employed people
in total employment drops to 10%. In fact, in France, this sector is one
of the privileged employment areas for the reintegration into work of
people who are covered by social policies. Here too (as in Germany),
the chance to count on two sources of income, one derived from work
in the area of services, the other from the minimum income, guarantees a stable proportion of low-wage workers to be employed in services.
Whether it refers to mini-jobs or to social work encouraged through the
policy of tax reductions for families, the combination of poor work and
minimum income makes it possible to avoid the burden of costs. To
all intents and purposes, it represents an alternative to both the public
route, effectively displaced due to higher labour costs, and the private
route, with the double objective of creating a hybrid condition of low-
paid work and assistance to supplement low wages. One is to provide the
means to deliver services at a low cost to the government and users. On
the other hand, the aim is to support active participation in the labour
market, thus contributing to the increase of employment among the
most vulnerable groups within the population.

As far as Italy is concerned, before going into the details of the transformations and reforms that have determined the quantity and quality
of employment development in personal care services, we can already
say that compared to France and Germany, we are faced with a very
different case. Not only because of the lack of a national policy to fight
poverty until more recent years, but also because of the lack of connection between social services and measures aimed at regularising undeclared work.

4.3 The Italian case: a fragmented welfare system without a recalibration strategy

The comparison with France and Germany is particularly important for
Italy. First of all, because of the many common features from the historical evolution of their welfare systems: from the emphasis on insurance schemes to protect employees, to the weakness and fragmentary
approach to assistance and, on the other hand, a significant burden
of responsibility on families. But if this was true in the past, it is not
the case in more recent years, in particular for care services. On the
other hand, in Italy, in spite of reforms – 328/2000 in particular – the
system of services has remained stuck in more traditional balances, on
the one hand with low spending on social policies and on the other
with a persistent overload of care tasks on the family. This weakness of

services is balanced by the strong commitment of families, but with negative consequences in terms of labour market participation, especially for women.

Moreover, undeclared work, often facilitated by the institutional system, remains widespread. Just think of the non-self-sufficiency and accompaniment allowance, a universal transfer (not subject to means-testing) that alone absorbed 13.6 billion – 0.81% of GDP in 2016 (INPS 2017). It is by far Italy's main welfare institution, largely benefiting the elderly (two-thirds of the beneficiaries), even though it is extended to the entire non-self-sufficient population. However, at present, its functioning is heavily conditioned by criticalities on several fronts, not only because of the absence of needs assessment grids organised on several levels (with each level corresponding to a different amount of resources for the beneficiaries, as is the case in the vast majority of European countries) but also because of the lack of dedicated procedures for the regularisation of informal work. In other words, the management of this institution lacks a system aimed at regularising informal care relationships (be they provided by a family member or a carer) or the procurement of services on a regular care market (Da Roit and Weicht 2013).

From this perspective, the Indennità di Accompagnamento reproduces a model of intervention based on transfers to families (as is traditional in Mediterranean welfare states) without any form of control over the use of these resources, nor tax incentive mechanisms for the recognition of informal care work or the emerging home-based workers. A few years ago, Pasquinelli and Rusmini (2013) estimated the number of irregular jobs in the care sector (mostly immigrant women) at 830,000, powered by the accompaniment allowance as well as by private household resources. Other authors have also highlighted this problem (Favarque 2013; see also León and Pavolini 2014), placing Italy among the European countries (together with Spain and Portugal) with the highest share of undeclared work in care services. In such a framework, rather than explicit policies aimed at creating new regular employment, it has been more often the recurrent regularisation programmes in favour of irregular immigrants (as many as three between 2002 and 2012) that have partly contributed to the emergence of undeclared work in care services. As León and Pavolini (2014) have written, the care work market in Italy is divided between regularisations indirectly recognising the role of immigrant workers and the substantial acceptance of irregular work within families. Despite these critical issues, the formal supply of care services provided by both not-for profit and for-profit providers has increased in recent years.

However, the circumstances under which the welfare supply has developed remain very inconsistent. As an example, consider the tax and contribution incentive measures for the purchase of home-based services that have been attempted to promote in recent years. The voucher affair for casual work is representative. Compared to what happened in other countries, for example, France with the CESU, the use of vouchers was not tailored to a specific sector (care and personal assistance) but concerned a broad spectrum of occasional and casual services, from personal services to trade and tourism. Initially introduced in agriculture, these vouchers (for a salary of 450 euros per month without contributions, the same level as German mini-jobs) were extended to many other sectors, until they reached considerable high rates in the final period before their definitive abrogation in 2017. As proof of this lack of focus on care services, consider that the employment created with this instrument in domestic services was rather low, compared to other sectors (trade, agriculture, and tourism), and to the much higher number of domestic workers registered with Inps, about 890 thousand in 2014 (see Figure 4.2). But more than vouchers or tax credits, the regularisation programmes and amnesties mentioned earlier have had an impact, given the large incidence of immigrant workers.

Regarding casual work, we can say that it represented the Italian version of the German mini-jobs, firstly because of the established wage level (the same and without contribution payments), and secondly because of the large scale of sectors in which it was applied. However, unlike in Germany, this push for low-paid jobs and low-end services was not accompanied by the reform of the minimum income, as in Germany. Due to the strong opposition of trade unions (with the threat of an abrogative referendum) casual work was abolished in 2017, just when the reform process that led first to the Reddito di Inclusione and then to the Reddito di Cittadinanza began. With the new centre-right government taking office at the end of 2022, a major revision of the Citizenship Income is underway. As of

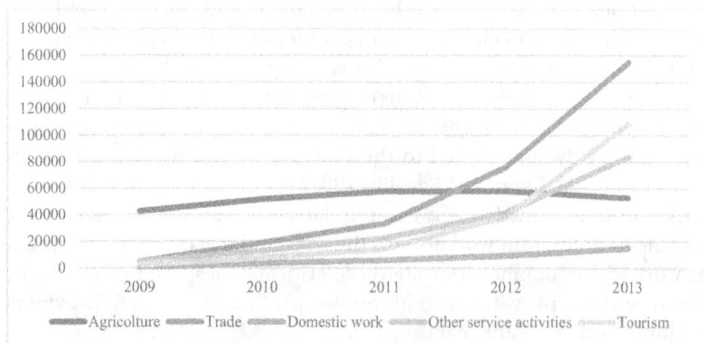

Figure 4.2 The impact of casual work vouchers on the labour market, Val. ass. Years 2009–2013

Source: Inps – Observatory on Domestic Work

2024, the Italian minimum income is supposed to split into two different instruments, one welfare aimed at the non-employable poor, the other for employable beneficiaries. For the latter, the subsidy will be significantly reduced through a work-first tightening of labour insertion measures.

In general terms, in Italy, neither the French nor the German model was adopted. Rather, reforms have been undertaken in a random order, without a clear orientation, ranging from categorical bonuses of varying sizes (Bonus bebè, Bonus asilo nido, Bonus per la nascita and birth support funds) to promoting corporate welfare. Over the past few years, it is above all on these complementary instruments negotiated within companies and at the sectoral level that the legislator's greatest attention has been focused in order to strengthen the welfare of services. The driving force was 2016, 2017, and 2018 Stability Laws, which introduced changes to productivity bonuses, extending their scope also through vouchers for access to fringe benefits at company level. Previously, the tax advantage was linked to a unilateral disbursement by the company to employees. Converting the productivity bonus into accredited welfare services has triggered intense bargaining activity at the company and sectoral level, resulting in an exchange between salaries and integrative services that involves two opposite logics. On the one hand, the restriction of public welfare and the difficulties in extending interventions toward the new social risks lead to decentralised negotiation (both at the sectoral and company level) to intervene in areas that were formerly a public area of competence. On the other hand, companies' requests for wage moderation pushed social partners to compensate with supplementary welfare for the loss of collective bargaining's influence on wages (Pavolini et al. 2013). Within this framework, many welfare issues have entered into collective bargaining instruments, at the sectoral, company, and even territorial levels. All this takes place within representation arrangements that are, on the one hand, more decentralised, and, on the other hand, also more segmented, between large or small companies, between sectors, between individual territorial areas, between permanently employed workers and those who are more marginalised in the labour market, precarious, or employed with contracts detached from integrative bargaining (Pavolini et al. 2013).

To date, the development of social services, whether contract-based (company or sector-based) or reflecting the offer of local authorities, remains fragmented, without a clear integration strategy, often left to specific territorial initiatives rather than a national plan (Maino and Rizza 2018). Successive reforms have produced sectoral interventions – often of limited duration – disconnected from an investment plan also on social infrastructures. Given a poor national coverage in terms of services, mainly characterised by strong and persistent territorial disparities (with the southern regions at clearly unsatisfactory levels compared to the number of potential beneficiaries), the lack of long-term prospects undermines the efforts and weakens the impact of the introduced measures.

4.4 Conclusions

The Italian model, among those examined, is the one that shows the least signs of renewal. In spite of multiple sectoral interventions and the growth of more structured service packages in some regions, an imbalance in support for traditional welfare measures persists in this country, oriented neither to regularising informal work nor to promoting direct job creation, albeit at low wages, in formal services. Instead, in many cases, social policies have ended up increasing undeclared work. The other countries analysed here (France and Germany) have pursued strategies with much more defined, albeit differentiated, guidelines: Germany aims at a broad distribution of low-cost (and low-wage) jobs through mini-jobs and a strategy of compressing labour costs in in-kind services; France uses the voucher system and tax breaks to encourage the creation of regular, but low-wage, work within families.

These policy choices, amidst the need to guarantee a greater range of social services in response to increasingly complex and multidimensional needs and the weight of budgetary constraints, have certainly made it possible to strengthen the system of social services, also (indirectly) incentivising female participation in the labour market. However, this has come at the price of a sharp increase in poor jobs in these services themselves, so much so that many of the social workers are beneficiaries of minimum income schemes. Since public expenditure and public employment cannot be trusted (at least within a certain limit), this trade-off appears as a structural fact, likely to become even stronger. Is there, therefore, no other option? With respect to the problem of undeclared work vouchers, tax relief and even the system of mini-jobs are preferable to the black economy, certainly for the state, which in this way can guarantee a broader tax and contribution base. On the other hand, especially in times of declining public resources, the problem of poorly paid labour is not solved. But this is not only a national problem. At the European level, even the European Commission has encouraged the implementation of tax reductions and deductions in order to lower the gross labour cost and encourage the creation of regular work within families. On the other hand, the ambitious objectives of social infrastructure and strengthening the European social model, most recently with the launch of the Social Pillar, are still without a specific budget or an ad hoc investment programme. In the absence of dedicated budget lines, the increase in the levels of supply and coverage of social services risks taking place affecting the quality of services or, even worse, compressing social workers' rights and protection.

References

Angermann, A., Eichhorst, W. (2012) *Eldercare Services – Lessons from a European Comparison.* Working Paper No. 6 of the Observatory for Sociopolitical Developments in Europe: IZA Research Report, n. 45, Bonn, June.

Bettio, F., Mazzotta, F. (2011) The future of care in Europe. Exploring the trade-offs that are driving change, in Kurswechsel. *Journal of the Committee for Socioeconomic and Environmental Alternatives,* 4, pp. 36–48.

Bode, I., Chartrand, S. (2011) *Home Care Provision in Germany. The State of Things and Recent Developments, Care Regimes on the Move in Europe.* Kassel: Institute of Social Work and Social Welfare, Dpt. 2 Universitaat Kassel.

Bonoli, G. (2005) The politics of the new social policies: providing coverage against new social risks in mature welfare states. *Policy & Politics,* 33(3), pp. 431–449.

Bonoli, G., Natali, D. (2012) *The Politics of the New Welfare State.* Oxford: Oxford University. Press.

Carbonnier, C., Morel N. (eds.) (2015) *The Political Economy of Household Services in Europe.* Basingstoke: Palgrave Macmillan.

Ciarini, A. (2016) Policies to boost services and employment in the long-term care sector. A downward convergence towards low-wage service jobs in the European welfare state? *Stato e Mercato,* 1, pp. 119–151.

Colombo, F., Nozal, A.L., Mercier, J., Tjadens, F. (2011) *Help Wanted? Providing and Paying for LTC.* Paris: OECD Health Policy Studies.

Cour des Compte. (2014) *Le développement des services à la personne et le maintien à domicile des personnes âgées en perte d'autonomie* (Enquête demandée par le Comité d'évaluation et de contrôle des politiques publiques de l'Assemblée Nationale). Paris: Juillet 2014.

Dares. (2018a) *Les salariés des services à la personne: comment évoluent leurs conditions de travail et d'emploi?* Paris: Dares Analyses.

Dares. (2018b) *Les services à la personne en 2016. L'activité se stabilise.* Paris: Dares Analyses.

Da Roit B., Weicht B. (2013) Migrant care work and care, migration and employment regimes: A fuzzy-set analysis. *Journal of European Social Policy,* 5, pp. 469–486.

Devetter, F.X., Lefebvre, M. (2015) Employment quality in the sector of personal and household services: Status and impact of public policies in France. In: Carbonnier, C., Morel, N. (eds) *The Political Economy of Household Services in Europe.* London: Palgrave Macmillan, pp. 150–172.

Drees. (2014) *Le compte de la dépendance en 2011 et à l'horizon 2060.* Dossiers solidarité et santé, 50, Paris.

Drees. (2019) *Minima sociaux et prestations sociales. Ménage aux revenues modestes et redistribution.* Paris: Edition 2018.

Eichhorst, W., Marx, P. (2012) Whatever works: Dualisation and the service economy in Bismarckian welfare states. In: Emmenegger, P., Häusermann, S., Palier, B., Seeleib-Kaise, M. (eds) *The Age of Dualization: The Changing Face of Inequality in Deindustrializing Societies.* Oxford: Oxford University Press, pp. 73–99.

Eichhorst, W., Marx, P.E., Tobsch, V. (2013) *Non-Standard Employment across Occupationsin Germany: The Role of Replaceability and Labour Market*

Flexibility. Discussion Paper, n. 7662, Institute for the Study of Labor (IZA), Bonn, October.

Esping-Andersen, G. (2000) *I fondamenti sociali delle economie postindustriali*. Bologna: il Mulino.

Esping-Andersen, G., Hemerijck A.E., Gallie, D.E., Myles J. (eds) (2002) *Why We Need a New Welfare State*. Oxford: Oxford University Press.

Favarque, N. (2013) *Developing Personal and Household Services in the EU. A Focus on Housework Activities* (Report for the DG Employment). Brussels: Social Affairs and Inclusion.

Guiraudon, V., Ledoux, C. (2015) The politics of tax exemptions for household services in France. In: Carbonnier, C., Morel, N. (eds) *The Political Economy of Household Services in Europe*. Hoboken, NJ: Palgrave Macmillan, pp. 39–59.

Hemerijck, A. (2012) Toward a new social policy paradigm. In: Morel, N., Palier B., Palme, J. (eds) *Towards a Social Investment Welfare State? Ideas, Policies and Challenges*. Bristol: The Policy Press.

Hemerijck, A. (2013) *Changing Welfare States*. Oxford: Oxford University Press.

INPS. (2017) *XVI Rapporto annuale INPS*. Roma: INPS.

Iversen, T., Wren, A. (1998) Equality, employment, and budgetary restraint: The trilemma of the service economy. *World Politics*, 50(4), pp. 507–546.

Lebrun, J.F. (2015) *Les services à la persone (SAP o PHS in English) en France* (Presentazione Percorsi di Secondo welfare). Roma: Italia Camp.

León, M., Pavolini, E. (2014) Social investment' or back to 'familism': The impact of the economic crisis on family and care policies in Italy and Spain. *South European Society and Politics*, 19(3), pp. 353–369.

Maino, F., Rizza, R. (2018) Le piccole e medie imprese incontrano il welfare: nuove opportunità di tutela dei lavoratori e di crescita per l'azienda e il territorio? *Stato e Mercato*, 2, pp. 197–224.

Meagher, G., Szebehely, M. (2013) Long-term care in Sweden: Trends, actors, and consequences. In: Ranci, C., Pavolini, E. (eds) *Reforms in Long-Term Care Policies in Europe: Investigating Institutional Change and Social Impacts*. New York: Springer, pp. 55–78.

Pasquinelli, S., Rusmini, G. (2013) Quante sono le badanti in Italia. *Qualificare*, 37. www.qualificare.info/home.php?list=archivio&id=678

Pavolini, E., Mirabile, M.L., Ascoli, U. (2013) *Tempi moderni. Il welfare nelle aziende in Italia*. Bologna: Il Mulino.

Pierson, P. (2001) *The New Politics of the Welfare State*. Oxford: Oxford University Press.

Rothgang, H. (2011) Social insurance for long-term care: An evaluation of the German model. In: Costa-Font, J. (eds) *Reforming Long-term care in Europe*. Chichester: Wiley-Blackwell, pp. 78–102.

Schmid, G. (2018) *Inclusive Growth: The Case of Germany*. IZA Policy Paper, n. 139, June.

Simonazzi, A.M., Picchi, S. (2013) Affordability of care and quality of work: New trends in elderly care. In: Bettio, F., Plantenga, J., Smith, M. (eds) *Gender and the European Labour Market*. London: Routledge, pp. 108–132.

5 Social investment recovery for a resilient Eurozone

Anton Hemerijck and Stefano Ronchi

5.1 European welfare states: beyond the equality-efficiency trade-off

The welfare state is perhaps the most successful feat of mid-20th-century social engineering. Since the Second World War, West-European welfare states virtually eradicated old-age poverty, provided universal access to health care and education, and institutionalized social security in case of unemployment and sickness. Over the last 50 years, however, welfare states have been faced with two complementary sets of challenges: in the first place, the social challenges coming from the changing nature of (gendered) risks in ageing post-industrial societies required a re-thinking of social policy. Second, the economic challenges coming from globalization, EU market integration, rapid technological innovation, intensified migration, and – not least – the Great Recession cast doubts on the sustainability of the welfare state as we know it.

In the final quarter of the 20th century, the tension between welfare states' social and economic priorities was predominantly described as irreconcilable. In the mid-1970s, the American economist Arthur Okun coined the 'big trade-off' between equality and efficiency (Okun 1975). To the extent that welfare spending is used as a political instrument to reduce inequality and relative poverty, Okun argued that this harms economic growth because of the income and labour market distortions produced by comprehensive social protection. In the mid-1990s, the OECD Jobs Study exposed the 'dark side' of double-digit unemployment in many of its West European members at the time (OECD 1994). Unemployment rates in France, Germany, and Italy were twice as high as in the United States, while their employment rates were well below US levels. Generous European welfare states thus seemed to incur economic stagnation. Against this backdrop, welfare retrenchment seemed the only way to allow for more efficient labour market allocation, although at the cost of somewhat greater income inequality. As Figure 5.1 reveals, however, this predicament has not proved inescapable.

DOI: 10.4324/9781003369707-5

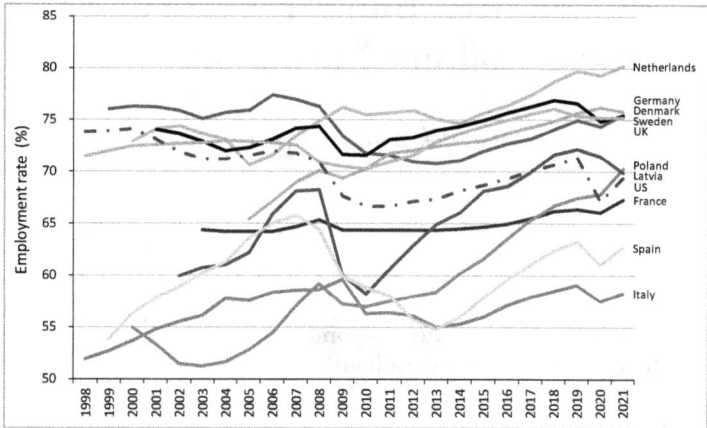

Figure 5.1 Employment trends in the United States and in ten selected European
countries (1998–2017)

Source: OECD

Figure 5.1 compares the employment trends of the United States
with those of ten selected European countries. At the end of the 1990s,
the United States held a record employment level of about 74%; only a
few northern European countries, like Denmark in the figure, were doing better. Subsequently, socioeconomic fortunes turned. Employment
in the United States went down, plummeting with the onslaught of the
financial crisis. When the COVID-19 pandemic broke, it had not (yet)
fully recovered. Today, the United States is no longer the champion of
high employment, even though unemployment is low. European countries, such as the Netherlands, Sweden, Germany, Denmark, and the
United Kingdom, do much better. With the exceptions of employment
stagnation in France, Italy, and Spain most European countries seem to
have found a way to escape the 'welfare without work' dilemma (Esping-
Andersen 1996).

Contrary to what Okun would have predicted, the new European
employment miracle was not accompanied by higher inequality and did
not come about on the ticket of welfare retrenchment. The trade-off
between economic efficiency and social equality no longer seems to
apply to advanced 21st-century knowledge economies in ageing societies. As recent research has shown (for a review, see Hemerijck and
Ronchi 2021), it is in fact some of the world's biggest welfare spenders –
namely northern European countries like Denmark, Sweden, and
Finland, but also continental welfare states such as Austria, Germany,

and the Netherlands – that perform best in terms of both equality *and* employment levels. If anything, Okun's trade-off appears as the exception rather than the rule, with two minimal 'liberal' welfare states such as the United States and, to a lesser extent, to the United Kingdom displaying relatively high but stagnating employment whilst performing poorly in terms of equality. To be sure, employment-equity success does not hold for all large European welfare states. Some big welfare spenders, such as France and Belgium, seemingly do well in terms of redistribution but have failed to raise employment levels. More worryingly, southern European countries fall short of both objectives: they face low employment and high levels of inequality despite sizable welfare spending ratios.

The variegated socioeconomic performance of European welfare states raises salient questions for the future of the E(M)U. A problematic divergence is taking hold of the European Union as not all member states managed to turn Okun's conjectured trade-off into a positive-sum solution. Those that did are the ones that have pursued social investment reform strategies, that is, they have recast and complemented established social protection programmes with employment- and family-friendly social policies. The same cannot be said for EU countries with low employment levels in Figure 5.1, which have instead declined to venture a social investment turn (Hemerijck and Ronchi 2021). Two lessons follow from this snapshot overview. For one, the 1980 and 1990s recipes of deregulation, liberalization and retrenchment have not proven to be sufficient to upkeep employment (let alone equality) in today's knowledge economies and ageing societies. Second, the experience of southern European social investment 'laggards' exposed that compensatory social protection also falls short of ensuring social inclusion and welfare sustainability. Investing in human capital and capabilities, while easing the flow of labour market and life-course transitions (think, for example, of work-family reconciliation) has become at least as important as buffering unemployment and poverty through income protection and compensation.

Pre-existing divergences between EU member states became deeper after the Great Recession, and they were further exacerbated by the socio-economic fallout of the COVID-19 pandemic (Kvist 2013; Heidenreich 2016; Claeys et al. 2021; Natili et al. 2022). During the 2010s, social investment-oriented welfare states had best been able to cushion the social and unemployment shocks. However, the stringency of the EMU fiscal governance framework, which was toughened in the Euro crisis, left countries in dire fiscal straits – yet most in need of social investment – reform with little option but to succumb to austerity and welfare retrenchment (Petmesidou and Guillén 2014). The music surely changed in the aftermath of the COVID-19 pandemic. The European policy response to unprecedented exogenous health shock marked a turn away from the austerity reflex of the previous decade. The Next Generation EU (NGEU) recovery plan adopted in July 2020 gives pride of place to public investments to relaunch growth, backed by the issuance of the first common EU debt, measuring up to a Hamiltonian moment of fiscal solidarity for the EU. This has surely reinforced a social investment impulse across the EU and not just in member-states with deep fiscal pockets. It should be recognized, however, that recent advancements in the economic governance, including mechanism to Support to Mitigate Unemployment Risks in an Emergency (SURE) of the EU, are all temporary in their nature. In the wake of the Ukrainian crisis, it is imperative to consolidate the EU fiscal stance to reinforce upward economic convergence and social progress in a still fragile Eurozone.

This chapter highlights the potential of social investment as a new paradigm for making 21st-century European welfare states both socially inclusive and economically sustainable in the post-crisis EU. The Section 5.2 revisits the analytical underpinnings of social investment along three interrelated policy functions of *lifelong human capital stock development, gender-balanced work-life flows* and *inclusive buffers*. Section three draws several key lessons from how the Euro crisis and the Great Recession impacted on diverse European welfare states. Section four uncovers the predicament of the E(M)U, epitomized by its schizophrenic Janus-face of being a social investment 'cheerleader' and fiscal austerity 'headmaster' in the same instance, especially in the years of the Euro crisis. It also highlights recent steps taken by the European Union towards the (re-)appreciation of social rights and public investment. The last section reflects on how new instruments like SURE and the Resilience and Recovery Facility (RFF), if put on a more permanent fiscal footing, may foster economic and social progress in tandem.

5.2 Rethinking the analytical underpinnings of social investment

Since 2000, before the crisis struck, the notion of social investment gained considerable purchase as a novel welfare compass to address exogenous economic dynamics and endogenous social change in an integrated fashion. European welfare states all share a basic common legacy, which dates to the 'Golden age' of economic as well as welfare growth in the post-war decades. The postwar welfare state of male-breadwinner full employment, female-homemaking, and high fertility was predominantly anchored on the function of income maintenance. Since the 1970s, external economic and endogenous social change weakened the foundations of post-war social contracts. Notwithstanding irreversible pressures, European welfare states did not fall prey to liberalizing retrenchment (Pierson 2001). Instead, to varying degrees, different welfare states experienced manifold attempts to rebuild social programmes in line with the evolving needs of post-industrial economies and societies (Taylor-Gooby 2004; Armingeon and Bonoli 2006; Bonoli and Natali 2012; Hemerijck 2013).

The post-industrial welfare state, catering for dual-earner families under far more adverse demographic conditions, requires welfare policy to reach beyond income provision in the 'here-and-now'. In the face of fast-changing social risks and needs, it ought to guarantee equitable resources with a 'capacitating' emphasis on the human capabilities needed to participate in social and economic life, to allow women to work and have children without being penalized, to eliminate skill deficiencies through lifelong education and training (beginning in early childhood), and to contain poverty, again, especially in early life, as child poverty easily perpetuates into adulthood. The 'capacitating' emphasis on providing households and individuals with a bundle of secure capabilities should not be misunderstood as a denunciation of income security. The experience of the Great Recession has, once again, underscored how important household income protection at the micro-level and demand stabilization at the macro-level remain in times of recession. Yet, for the post-industrial context of intensified knowledge competition, demographic ageing, and gender change, the foundational social security buffer function of the welfare state must be complemented and aligned with more proactive capacitating policy functions.

This is where social investment approach gains importance, as it underlines the provision of high-quality social services, with a focus on *stocks* and *flows,* alongside elementary social security *buffers.* Post-industrial welfare provision can now be conceptualized in terms of three complementary policy functions: (1) raising and maintaining the 'stock' of human capital and capabilities throughout the life course (*lifelong human capital stocks*); (2) easing the 'flow' of gendered labour market and life-course transitions (*work-life-balanced flows*); and (3) granting inclusive safety nets (*inclusive buffers*). In day-to-day policy practice, there is considerable overlap between the different welfare functions of stocks, flows and buffers. Policy provisions that at face value privilege one of the three functions typically also back up the other functions in an interconnected fashion. Seen from the perspective of 'institutional complementarities', poverty alleviation, principally a 'buffering' policy, can smooth labour market flow, because of mitigated pressure and background financial stability to accept quality (and not any) job on offer, with the potential benefit of better job-matching and less human capital stock depletion. By the same token, childcare stock-investment also facilitates labour market flows for working parents.

Policies such as early childhood education and care (ECEC); education and training over the life course; active labour market policies

(ALMP); work-life balance (WLB) policies such as parental leave and flexible employment relations; lifelong learning (LLL); and long-term care (LTC) all share the objectives of enhancing people's capabilities and opportunities in post-industrial labour markets, with a view to ensuring high levels of gender-equitable employment, social cohesion, individual autonomy, and overall life satisfaction. In addition to the material wellbeing returns for programme beneficiaries, social investment policies have the capacity to increase the number (*quantity*) and productivity (*quality*) of current and future employees (Myles 2002; Hemerijck 2017). To the extent that welfare provision in a knowledge economy is geared towards maximizing employment, employability, and productivity, this serves to sustain the so-called 'carrying capacity' of the modern welfare state – the lynchpin of the social investment edifice (Myles 2002). From this perspective, employment is the core lubricant in the carrying capacity of mature welfare state, as social policy provision is largely paid for by income taxes and social contributions (Hemerijck 2018). Aggregate evidence on welfare performance – before and after the crisis – corroborates the effectiveness of social investment: countries with strong and integrated portfolios of *stock, flow*, and *buffer* policies are best able to reconcile economic competitiveness and social inclusion (Hemerijck 2013, 2017; Hemerijck and Matsaganis, forthcoming).

Mounting evidence on how effective *stock, flow*, and *buffer* policies reinforce each other has inspired the conjecture of a social investment 'life-course multiplier', whereby cumulative social investment returns over the life-course plausibly generate a cycle of well-being in terms of employment opportunities, gender equity, and a significant mitigation of intergenerational poverty (Hemerijck 2017: 26). This virtuous cycle begins from early investments in children through high quality ECEC, which translate into higher levels of educational attainment, which in turn, together with more tailor-made vocational training, spills over into higher and more productive employment in the medium term (Brilli et al. 2016; Heckman 2006; Cunha and Heckman 2007). To the extent that employment participation is furthermore supported by effective work-life balance policies, including adequately funded and publicly available childcare, higher levels of (female) employment with lower gender pay and employment gaps can be foreseen (Del Boca et al. 2005; Nieuwenhuis et al. 2012; Korpi et al. 2013; Plavgo and Hemerijck 2021). On top of protecting households against worklessness and poverty (Cantillon and Vandenbroucke 2014; Rovny 2014), more opportunities for women and men to combine parenting with paid labor, moreover, is likely to bolster fertility at a time when (young) couples struggle to reconcile family aspirations with uncertain working times and income guarantees (Bernardi 2005). A final knock-on effect is a higher effective retirement age, provided the availability of active ageing policies, including portable and flexible pensions, supported also by long-term care policies to secure on-going (female) employment participation of late career adults with frail elders (Kuitto and Helmdag 2021). Higher and more productive employment implies a larger tax base to sustain the carrying capacity of the welfare state, thus squaring the circle of the social investment multiplier function.

5.3 Six policy lessons from the Great Recession

Although starting from different institutional legacies, all EU welfare states have been engaged in adjusting policy provision to upkeep human capital and employment levels. Based on the differences in economic vulnerability, administrative capacity, reform timing and urgency, and intensity of welfare adaptations, European countries can be grouped into five clusters of social investment reform trajectories (Hemerijck and Ronchi 2021):

1 'Vanguard' countries like Denmark and Sweden shifted towards a social investment-oriented rebalance of stock-flow-buffer functions well ahead of other countries.
2 Other countries, such as the United Kingdom and the Netherlands, jumped (or tried to jump) on the active-inclusion 'bandwagon' in the 1990s, and did so by starting from different welfare settings.
3 'Latecomers' such as Germany and Spain, introduced social investment reforms in some policy domains later on, in the 2000s, again from different institutional starting blocks.
4 Social investment 'laggards' did less, almost without reforming their arrangements of stock, flow and buffer policies (e.g. France and Italy).
5 'Newcomers' – new EU member states in Eastern Europe – had to rapidly adjust former socialist welfare provision to multiple post-transition challenges, and, in varying ways, picked up selectively on some social investment imperatives (Avlijaš 2022).

Having developed along these variegated trajectories, European welfare states came to the outbreak of the global financial crisis with profoundly different stock-flow-buffer arrangements. While some proved effective in cushioning the economic and social shocks produced by the crisis, others were unable to contain the outburst of unemployment, poverty and social exclusion. Moreover, the widespread turn to austerity which followed the Euro crisis not only hindered the progress of social investment but also induced policy reversal in some countries that had started to take that reform trajectory in the 2000s. More than ten years after the Great Recession, we can draw several fundamental policy lessons for the prospects of social investment in 21st-century Europe. Some of them have been reinforced in the aftermath during the COVID crisis, when not only governments and citizens rediscovered how fundamental healthcare, employment maintenance schemes, and many other welfare programmes are for buffering social risks, but EU countries also realized that countercyclical spending and public investment must chip for reasons of stabilization, whilst buying precious time to develop effective vaccines. Taken as a whole, these lessons entail good news for social investment, thus giving us a 'glass half-full' image of the policy blueprint. Other lessons, however, make the glass look half empty, and raise gloomier prospects on the viability of a truly inclusive social investment agenda for the entire European Union if today's EMU governance framework remains unchanged. We summarize these policy lessons in the six points that follows.

(1) *Overall, the last two decades of welfare reform have witnessed a general move towards social investment, although this trend was interrupted by the conservative austerity reflex that followed the Euro crisis.* Before the crisis struck, with few exceptions (such as Italy and Greece), social investment recalibration had become the *fil rouge* in welfare reform among Europe's mature welfare states. Policymakers in these countries recognized that, in the face of intensified demographic ageing and disruptive technological change, future economic growth will rely heavily on high levels of employment and improvements in productivity. Today there is ample proof that social investments in child-care, long-term care, education and training, active labour market policy, lifelong learning and active ageing, paid parental leave, family services and benefits, in a complementary fashion, significantly contribute to (female) employment, productivity, demographic balance, improved fertility, increased tax revenue, reduced long-term reliance on compensatory social protection policies, and lower worklessness – one of the main determinants of poverty (for a review, Hemerijck 2017). Unsurprisingly, the Nordic countries, which have independent currencies, inclusive safety nets, and strong social service traditions, have done the most to protect social investment progress. By contrast, Eurozone countries, having to abide by the Stability and Growth Pact's (SGP) deficit rule of 3% and public debt of 60% of GDP, took a back seat on social investment reform (see, for example, Ólafsson et al. 2019; Hemerijck and Matsaganis forthcoming) nordic welfare states today outperform the liberal and continental welfare states on employment, productivity, dual earner families, gender equality, (child-)poverty, and fiscal balance. By 2020, in terms of early-childhood stock development and work-life flow provision, the German welfare state

as a social investment latecomer overtook the bandwagoners of the Netherlands and the United Kingdom. In these two countries, social investment progress stalled. Both countries experimented with the provision of private, yet publicly subsidized, Early Childhood Education and Care (ECEC). Based on these experiences. Although this spurred a massive expansion of childcare provision, private provision, compensated by tax benefits to ensure distributive fairness in access to young families, ignited a perverse dynamic of ever-escalating fees in these countries, without significant (educational) quality improvement in ECEC (Hemerijck and Matsaganis, forthcoming).

(2) *Automatic stabilizers work, and so does social investment in acting as a kind of ex ante 'employment shock absorber' that reduces job loss in a preventative fashion.* The Great Recession was triggered by a financial crisis, just like the Great Depression, and not by a stagflation real-economy crisis as in the 1970s and 1980s. This macroeconomic predicament conjured up a test-case for the legacy of Keynesian-Beveridgean welfare state. Built on compulsory social insurance, the latter acts as an 'automatic stabilizer' in times of recession, cushioning the crisis through anti-cyclical consumption smoothing (i.e. unemployment benefits offering income-support to those who lose their jobs). By and large, automatic-stabilization social security, largely absent in the 1930s, provided the largest stimulus in most countries while protecting household income after 2008 (Armingeon 2012). What is even more interesting, for it constitutes the real novelty of post-industrial welfare states facing the first economic crisis of the 21st century, is the capacity that social investment showed in cushioning the employment shock in the first place, that is, by limiting job destruction (or boosting re-employment chances) so as to shore up employment before the need for traditional automatic stabilizers to intervene. While the employment prospects of people living in countries that spend more on social investment remained almost constant throughout the crisis years, they deteriorated drastically for those living in countries less inclined to social investment (Ronchi 2019; see also Nelson and Stephens 2012 and Bakker and Van Vliet 2021 on the employment-enhancing potential of social investment).

(3) *Positive institutional complementarities emerge between social investment policies and more traditional social protection policies.* To wit, social investment works better when supported by inclusive social protection 'buffers', and *vice versa.* Such complementarities between diverse social policies have recently become subject of empirical analysis (Hemerijck et al. 2016; Bakker and Van Vliet 2021; Plavgo and Hemerijck 2021), which showed, for example, how higher public

spending on social investment reduces the work-disincentive which is sometimes – though not always (Lehwess-Litzmann and Nicaise 2020) – attached to out-of-work cash-transfers to the unemployed (Ronchi 2019). By the same token, the 'Matthew effects' which are often attributed to social investment (i.e. unintended inequality-reinforcing outcomes that disproportionally benefit the middle class (Bonoli et al. 2017) result somewhat mitigated where 'buffer' policies are more generous, and other policy complementarities are observable among specific vulnerable social groups (Hemerijck et al. 2016; Ronchi 2019; Bakker and Van Vliet 2021; Plavgo and Hemerijck 2021; Rovny 2014).

The first three lessons from the Great Recession show that 'social investment works'! There are others that are less sanguine, turning the good news above into a glass half-empty.

(4) *Social investment recalibration was hardly viable within the narrower fiscal space left by post-crisis austerity.* After the outbreak of the Euro crisis, social investment reform came to a halt in most member states, even in those which embarked on that policy path in early-2000s (Petmesidou and Guillén 2014; Bouget et al. 2015; Ronchi 2018). Those countries, lacking effective stocks and flows, that would benefit most from effective social investment, were put on the diet of welfare austerity. Overall, even despite the possibility to activate of the escape clause of the SGP (see Section 5.4), the fiscal space available to governments in fiscal dire straits heavily constrained social investment responses, also in the immediate aftermath of the COVID crisis. Despite having been hit hardest by the COVID-19 pandemic, high-debt countries like Italy and Spain could not deploy a fiscal response comparable to the big 'fiscal bazooka' of Germany (Moreira et al. 2021; Natili et al. 2022). Eurozone already problematic divergences coming out of the financial crisis risked being deepened in the aftermath of the pandemic, at a time when repeated economic and social crises seemingly transmuted into an even deep political crisis of the European integration project.

(5) *Policy* in-*complementarities persist in those welfare states that did not reform before the Great Recession, and that found it hard to raise the reform perspective of social investment afterwards.* As argued earlier, many countries of the EU are far from having balanced portfolios of stock, flow and buffer policies. In times of austerity, policy complementarities are very hard to be put in place. Fiscal consolidation leaves little space for expanding single pieces of social policies, let alone for coordinated investments in multiple policy areas (e.g. ideally, expanding social investments in childcare and activation policies

while also making social protection buffers more inclusive). When they come in isolation, activation-only policy provisions can drift into *workfare* rather than truly inclusive social investment (Bonoli 2012), especially when they are not built on adequate minimum income guarantees. Work *per se* is not always a sufficient guarantee against poverty (Andress and Lohmann 2008). Finally, there is no such a thing as zero-cost investment in capacitating social services. Cheap services often mean low-quality services, based on poorly paid-poorly trained workers, or subcontracted to private providers who follows market prices, thus leading to social bias in access (the case, for example, of education and childcare policies in the United Kingdom and the Netherlands), in turn conducive to gendered Matthew effects (poor mothers prefer to stay home to take care of their children themselves instead of paying very expensive crèches).

(6) *Social investment has long-term effects, which clash with the short-term perspective of national politicians.* While cash transfers flows almost immediately to welfare recipients, it surely needs time to reap the fruits of investments in education, but also in work-family reconciliation and activation policies. As Maurizio Ferrera (2016) framed it, '[t]he temporal mismatch between social investment reforms and their returns requires a degree of 'political patience' on the side of both current voters and incumbent politicians which is not readily available in contemporary democracies'. For the time being, the potential of the European Union as 'social investment-policy facilitator' has been curtailed by the predominance of fiscal austerity across the E(M)U. After the Euro crisis outbreak, it became clear that Eurozone membership was not a blessing *per se*, and the inbuilt inconsistencies of the EMU favoured austerity and retrenchment rather than fostering upward recalibration towards social investment. Section 5.4 delves deeper into the somewhat schizophrenic stance that the European Union took in the early 2010s in respect to its long-time double commitment to economic prosperity and social progress.

5.4 Learning from past mistakes: beyond fair-weather social investment?

EU institutions, and especially the Commission, should be given credit for raising the stakes of social investment. Against the tide of fashionable tragic trade-offs, ever since the Amsterdam Summit of 1997, the European Commission has helped build the edifice of social investment, from the stepping-stones in the Lisbon Agenda of 2000 to a fully-fledged welfare paradigm with the publication of the Social Investment

Package in 2013, many recommendations of which have recently been codified in the 2017 Pillar of Social Rights. However, as much as the European Commission has become the world's 'social investment cheerleader', in the decade of the Euro crisis, the Barroso Commission fell back on a posture of 'fiscal austerity headmaster'. To be sure, the Italian predicament of low employment (recall Figure 5.1) and high poverty has home-grown roots. Yet, its perpetuation in the wake of the global financial crash is intimately related to how the Euro crisis, which came to a head in 2012, shaped different E(M)U welfare states' adjustment pathways. The original policy theory of the currency union was based on the assumption that the European Central Bank's (ECB) mandate on price stability, together with a strong commitment to fiscal consolidation enforced by the Stability and Growth Pact, would raise 'structural reform' pressures on the member states. In hindsight, the Eurozone crisis exposed the weakness of this naïve policy theory.

In the early years of the euro, Germany undershot the ECB's inflation target. At the same time, the Mediterranean countries and Ireland struggled with high inflation at fortuitous levels of catch-up growth. Although Spain and Ireland continued to adhere to fiscal conservatism, lower interest rates and easy credit stimulated a construction bubble, financed by a massive hike in private debt, which ultimately burst. For Italy and Greece, with their troubled public finances, a different scenario unfolded. After they had secured safe entry into the EMU, structural reform incentives waned as public borrowing grew excessively cheap. Paradoxically, the EMU acted as a 'reform tranquilizer', reducing rather than reinforcing pressures to enact structural reforms to bring their fiscal houses in order when they could. As a result, social investment welfare reform never took off where it was needed the most, in the Southern periphery characterized by insider-biased labour markets and male-breadwinner, pension-heavy welfare states. Politically, the aftermath of the Euro crisis caught governments in dire fiscal straits between Scylla and Charybdis. On the one hand, pressures for deficit reduction constrained the domestic policy space for social investment innovation. On the other hand, populist governments, successful with disenchanted electorates, increasingly decline to abide by austerity compromises made in Brussels. The 2018 Italian election is the case in point: the anti-establishment Five Star Movement formed a coalition government with the far right and xenophobic Lega, on a ticket of expanding compensatory social protection spending instead of capacitating social investments, and at the price of a higher deficit. The aftermath of the Euro crisis raised serious questions about whether the European social investment impetus could survive the clash between EMU-reinforced fiscal austerity and rising national (sometimes illiberal) populism.

On top of political backlashes, the austerity response to the Great Recession seemed to have got stuck in a perverse vicious cycle. To wit, the 'social imbalances' that rose throughout Europe in the 2010s were both the consequence of structural imbalances of the EMU, and, in turn, a likely cause of further instability in the same E(M)U (Vandenbroucke et al. 2013). In the first place, the deterioration of socioeconomic conditions observed in some countries was at least in part linked to the misalignment of the economic cycles and constrained by the fiscal stringency of EMU economic governance. Second, growing social imbalances was problematic for the EMU precisely because high levels of poverty (child poverty in particular) and the general depletion of human capital in peripheral countries (especially in the case of the potential 'scarring' effect of youth unemployment) could contribute to further widen economic divergence in the long term.

In hindsight, over the period 2010–2014, EU austerity remained to dominant show in town. With the entry Jean-Claude Juncker as Commission President, we can already observe considerable policy-reorientation, admittedly, on the wing of ECB's turn to 'whatever it takes' heterodox monetary policy in 2012, and the reappraisal of social investment proficiency as laid down in the 2013 Social Investment Package, masterminded by Social Affairs Commissioner László Andor. The gradual but transformative erosion of the austerity paradigm was layered by a path-shifting reorientation in the macroeconomics of the Eurozone (Hemerijck and Corti 2022). Change was reflected not only in a more flexible interpretation and implementation of the EU fiscal rules (Miró 2021) but also in a new understanding of the relationship between the E(M)U and nation-based welfare states, with the latter no longer being conceived as a negative 'adjustment variable' to achieve fiscal stability and cost-competitiveness (Costamagna 2019). Social policies were again re-appraised as productive factors, contributing to welfare states' carrying capacity, boosting competitiveness and growth by increasing workers productivity. Later, however, with the launch of the European Pillar of Social Rights (EPSR), a new more promising normative understanding of the welfare state functions, combining adequate safety nets, high-level investments in human capital and generous support services over the work-family life-course transitions, was translated into a list of 20 social rights and principles, combing already existing rights in the Union so-called *social acquis* and new ones addressing the challenges arising from societal, technological and economic developments. Politically, the proclamation of the Social Pillar was a turning point. It gave a new impetus to the further socialization of Country Specific Recommendation in the European semester and the promotion and adoption of new legislative and non-legislative initiatives (Garben 2019) from the work-life balance directive to the more recent directive on fair minimum wages, under Ursula von der Leyen as Commission President (Vesan et al. 2021). Still, with the Stability and Growth pact intact before the COVID-19 pandemic broke, the flexibility clause was hardly used (Darvas and Anderson 2020), while the reorientation of the Semester towards inclusive and resilient welfare states, remained a bit of a paper tiger, privileging social investment reforms countries with deep fiscal pockets rather than those in dire straits.

Against the backdrop of a changing *Zeitgeist*, it is not surprisingly that the European response to the COVID crisis in 2020 was profoundly different from the one entertained in the early days of the global financial crash (Ladi and Tsarouhas 2020). The combination of the peculiar traits of this new crisis – a devastating public health crisis with unprecedented diffuse social and economic consequences – and experiential learning from the mistakes made during the Euro crisis, accelerated EU institutions and policymakers to leapfrog towards a far more solidaristic approach facing the COVID crisis. As highlighted by Alcidi and Corti (2022), three quintessential 'taboos' were (temporarily) broken, thus opening the room for a debate on the future of post-COVID E(M)U economic governance. In the first place, the Commission activated the general escape clause of the Stability and Growth Pact, with a view to providing member states with more fiscal flexibility to pursue discretionary stimuli to support health and social spending and to protect their economies in the deep recession following national lockdowns and travel restrictions. The second broken taboo was the swift adoption of SURE (temporary Support to mitigate Unemployment Risks in an Emergency): an instrument to support national short-time work schemes (job retention programmes like *Kurzarbeit* in Germany, *Cassa integrazione* in Italy or The Spanish ERTE [*Expediente de Regulación Temporal de Empleo*], to quote just a few examples) through unconditional loans granted with favourable terms from the European Union to member states facing sudden increases in public expenditure for the preservation of employment. As such, SURE not only constituted an innovative inter-state redistributive mechanism but also marked the full backing of automatic stabilizers in times of recession on the side of the Commission. Last but not least, the other taboos to be broken in the context of the COVID crisis were the rediscovery of public investment as an instrument of growth and the issuance of common EU debt (Alcidi and Corti 2022). The latter is used to finance both the SURE programme and, most important, the broader NGEU recovery plan, which involved the European Commission undertaking massive borrowing on the capital markets for the first time (up to 750 billion euros) to provide grants (up to about 390 billion euros) and loans to economically weaker member states.

The fiscal space guaranteed by the NGEU plan, and the blueprint for industrial (the green and the digital transitions) and welfare reform set up in the framework of the Recovery and Resilience Facility (RRF), seem to credit much better incentives to put 'laggard' welfare states back on the track of post-industrial modernization. The RRF, at the heart of the NGEU package, has been widely appreciated as marking a critical juncture in the development of the EU towards a stronger redistributive function (Armingeon et al. 2022) and a clear break with austerity reflex of the early 2010s (Buti and Papakonstantinou 2021). There is also the explicit commitment in the RRF to enhance the Union's economic, social, and territorial cohesion and convergence beyond the mitigation of the socio-economic consequences of the COVID-19 crisis and to contribute to the implementation of the EPSR, thereby 'restoring and promoting sustainable growth and the integration of the economies of the Union, fostering high quality employment creation' (RRF Regulation, Art. 4).

Although it is early days, by glancing through national recovery programs, we can already observe that main-beneficiary southern European countries today are far more serious about social investment than ever before. Italy is planning to massively invest in ECEC and to strengthen Public Employment Services; Spain is committed to upgrade activation, vocational training, upskilling and reskilling policies; and Portugal will invest more in social housing and primary healthcare. By contrast, up north, the minor-beneficiary countries of Germany and the Netherlands are less committed to social investment, using the funds to already budgeted expenditure, which perhaps is a luxury they can afford as they fast-forwarded social investment reform at an earlier stage.

5.5 Making social investment a recovery priority in the Eurozone

Untried policy ideas are never expedient, but they become relevant when unanticipated political contingencies press status-quo-breaking politics. Any problem-solving search for a more balanced European socioeconomic governance regime should start with a proper diagnosis of the 2008 crash and its unexpected spillovers into the Eurozone crisis and the COVID-19 pandemic. Based on the theoretical and empirical considerations put forward in this chapter, our contention on this score is that Europe's most successful feat of mid-20th century social engineering – the national welfare state, a brainchild of the Great Depression – was wrongly (but not surprisingly) left in political disregard when the global financial crisis struck in 2008. The 'structural reform' mantra of labour market deregulation, social protection retrenchment, pension privatization and social service liberalization ruled the waves of Eurozone financial crisis management, widening divergence rather than nurturing upward convergence across the besieged continent. The overwhelming evidence that the more active – big spending – welfare states of north-western Europe were best able to absorb the economic and social aftershocks of the global credit crunch, and the Eurozone conundrum that followed suit, should really form the launching pad for exploring effective and legitimate post-crisis E(M)U and domestic reform complementarities.

The first E(M)U-reform proposal of this kind concerns the reinforcement the SURE capacity for the eurozone. Given that inclusive welfare states are far more robust at buffering asymmetric shocks, many economists and policy makers, among whom ex-commissioner László Andor and former Belgian social affairs and pensions minister Frank Vandenbroucke, have been instrumental in setting the agenda for the SURE 're-insurance' mechanism for national unemployment insurance systems to provide fiscal breathing space for countries asymmetrically affected by a possible downturn (Dullien 2014; Beblavý et al. 2015; Andor 2016; Vandenbroucke 2017; Vandenbroucke et al. 2017; Vandenbroucke et al. 2020). While SURE provides support to short-time work schemes (i.e. it is an instrument for retain jobs and prevent unemployment), the original proposal of a European unemployment benefit scheme (EUBS) would better address the broader objective of shoring up national income-compensation benefits for the unemployed. In Andor and Vandenbroucke's opinion, the supranational unemployment re-insurance scheme should focus on the eurozone, which seems reasonable insofar as the overriding – Keynesian – lesson from the European experience of the Great Recession was the non-availability of a policy instrument for eurozone shock absorption. There are practical problems with both SURE and EUBS. As Vandenbroucke (2017) conceded, any effective eurozone social reinsurance facility impinges on the variegated design of national unemployment insurance systems, especially regarding the extent to which the prevailing social security systems can buffer large cohorts in the working-age population. In other words, there is a clear need for some minimal institutional convergence in the scope and operational routines of national social insurance systems for a smooth Keynesian operation of the envisaged eurozone unemployment re-insurance, touching on social security coverage, activation, minimum wages and income protection for households with weak attachments to the labour market. An additional problem is that social (re-)insurance provision typically protects insiders rather than outsiders, this being even more true for the SURE instrument of short-time work support. Effective and more inclusive minimum income buffers continue to be crucial to provide social buffers to those who are outside of the coverage of social insurance (e.g. precarious workers with scattered employment records and low social contributions). From the perspective of current social imbalances, arguably, outsiders, ranging from youngsters, women, migrants and the long-term unemployed, rather than labour market insiders, disproportionately bear the brunt of the social after-shocks of the pandemic. Finally, and deeply connected to this, and al-though SURE already proved effective in the event of the pandemic, it cannot effectively address problems socioeconomic divergence, as the ones unleashed by the Euro crisis and its conservative austerity reflex.

In this respect, the RRF as it creates a genuine fiscal space that links investments to reforms, is far more promising (Corti 2022). Reasoning on the three policy functions of social investment in terms of a viable division of responsibilities between the EU and the member states, clearly the function of social security 'buffers', the core prerogative of the national welfare state, jealously guarded by domestic political ac-tors, should remain in the remit of national welfare provision, but can be supported by instruments of Eurozone reinsurance buffering. The 'flow' function, concerning labour market regulation and collective bargaining in synch with work-life balance, gender equality, and family-friendly employment relations, is best served by mutual learning and monitoring processes of open coordination, engaging national admin-istrations, relevant EU expert committees and social partners in sharing practices – good and bad – for reform inspiration. This leaves us with the overriding importance of the social investment 'stock' option. The Eurozone austerity reflex resulted in a public investment strike, most unfortunately in the area of human capital stock, early childhood and lifelong education and training, with significant negative spillovers for growth, employment and productivity in Europe's knowledge econo-mies facing adverse demographics. As we know, 'soft' investments in human capital concern discretionary expenditures that tend to be cut easily in times of austerity (Streeck and Mertens 2011). It is here that the RRF could deploy its fiscal weight without trespassing national wel-fare jealousies. Granting more fiscal room (within bounds) to countries that have experienced ominous social and macroeconomic imbalances would enable them to secure future-oriented financing of their lifelong education, skill upgrading, and social care systems before the ageing predicament becomes truly overwhelming. Especially for countries struggling to commit to a balanced budget without abandoning their 'buffering' social protection commitments, the RRF could foster im-mediate gains in early childhood, female employment, improved work-life balance and reduced levels of early school leaving, with positive medium-term outcomes in employment growth, productivity through higher educational attainment and ultimately a lower pension burden resulting from higher levels of employment. Moreover, because any hu-man capital upgrading strategy often takes a generation to fully reap the anticipated returns, a long-term commitment to social investment is finally shining through. Finally, there is a political responsibility attachment to the RRF. Policymakers in Italy, Spain, Portugal, Croatia, and Slovenia, understand full well that if fiscal solidarity is to be a permanent feature in the EU's future policy toolbox, the implementation of the national recovery plans must be a glaring success by the time the NGEU run out in 2026.

Yet, all that glistens isn't gold. By putting fiscal meat on the bones of the Semester CSRs, most definitely, the RRF opens a window of opportunity to finally translate the principles of the Social Pillar in the national social investment reform agendas. As the RRF is about capital expenditures, not current expenditures, there is the unresolved problem of a green light for stock/flow investments in day-care and training centres, with current expenditures of nursing and teachers' salaries still hemmed in by the SGP, risking the RRF to help build 'bridges to nowhere' (Bokhorst and Corti forthcoming). A more assertive EU-level social investment strategy with fiscal teeth that privileges both current and capital expenditures would be to exempt human capital infrastructural investments and stock-related current expenditures from the SGP by a 'Golden Rule' of – say – up to 1.5% of GDP (Hemerijck and Ronchi 2020). Admittedly, any Golden Rule requires an EU-level political agreement commitment to a privileged policy function or cause, facing risks of underinvestment, together with well-designed processes learning and monitoring policy feedback on the anticipated economic and social outcomes.

References

Alcidi, C. and Corti, F. (2022) The EU response to Covid-19: Breaking old taboos? In: Vanhercke, B., Spasova, S. (eds) *Social Policy in the European Union: State of Play 2021. Re-emerging Social Ambitions as the EU Recovers from the Pandemic.* Brussels: European Trade Union Institute (ETUI) and European Social Observatory (OSE), pp. 39–60.

Andor, L. (2016) Towards shared unemployment insurance in the euro area. *IZA Journal of European Labor Studies*, 5(10).

Andress, H.J., Lohmann, H. (eds) (2008) *The Working Poor in Europe: Employment, Poverty and Globalisation.* Cheltenham: Edward Elgar Publishing.

Armingeon, K. (2012) The politics of fiscal responses to the crisis of 2008–2009. *Governance*, 25(4), pp. 543–565.

Armingeon, K., Bonoli, G. (2006) *The Politics of Post-Industrial Welfare States: Adapting Post-War Social Policies to New Social Risks.* London and New York: Routledge.

Armingeon, K., de la Porte, H.C., Sacchi, S. (2022) Voices from the past: Economic and political vulnerabilities in the making of next generation EU. *Comparative European Politics*, 20(2), pp. 144–165.

Avlijaš, S. (2022) Explaining the contrasting welfare trajectories of the Baltic and Visegrád countries: A growth-strategy perspective. In: Garritzmann, J.L., Häusermann, S., Palier B. (eds) *The World Politics of Social Investment (Volume II): The Politics of Varying Social Investment Strategies.* Oxford: Oxford University Press, pp. 209–230.

Bakker, V., Van Vliet, O. (2021) Social investment, employment and policy and institutional complementarities: A comparative analysis across 26 OECD countries. *Journal of Social Policy*, 1–23.

Beblavý, M., Gros, D., Maselli, I. (2015) *Reinsurance of national unemployment benefit schemes. CEPS Working Document no. 401 (January, 2015)*. Brussels: Centre for European Policy Studies.

Bernardi, F. (2005) Public policies and low fertility: rationales for public intervention and a diagnosis for the Spanish case. *Journal of European Social Policy*, 15(2), pp. 123–138.

Bokhorst D. and Corti F. (forthcoming) Governing Europe's Recovery and Resilience Facility: Between discipline and discretion, *Government and Opposition*.

Bonoli, G. (2012) Active labour market policies and social investment: A changing relationship. In: Morel, N., Palier, B., & Palme, J. (eds) *Towards a Social Investment State*. Bristol: Policy Press, pp. 181–204.

Bonoli, G., Natali, D. (2012) *The Politics of the New Welfare State*. Oxford: Oxford University Press.

Bonoli, G., Cantillon, B., Van Lancker, W. (2017) Social investment and the Matthew effect: Limits to a strategy. In: Hemerijck, A. (ed) *The Uses of Social Investment*. Oxford: Oxford University Press.

Bouget, D., Frazer, H., Marlier, E., et al. (2015) *Social Investment in Europe. A Study of National Policies*. Brussels: European Commission, DG Employment, Social Affairs and Inclusion.

Brilli, Y., Del Boca, D., Pronzato, C.D. (2016) Does child care availability play a role in maternal employment and children's development? Evidence from Italy. *Review of Economics of the Household*, 14(1), pp. 27–51.

Buti, M., and Papakonstantinou, G. (2021) The legacy of the pandemic: How Covid-19 is reshaping economic policy in the EU, CEPR Policy Insight No. 109, April 2021.

Cantillon, B., Vandenbroucke, F. (2014) *Reconciling Work and Poverty Reduction: How Successful Are European Welfare States?* Oxford and New York: Oxford University Press.

Claeys, G., Darvas, Z., Demertzis, M., Wolff G.B. (2021) The great COVID-19 divergence: Managing a sustainable and equitable recovery in the EU. *Intereconomics*, 56(4), pp. 211–219.

Corti, F. (2022) *The politicisation of social Europe: conflict dynamics and welfare integration*. Cheltenham: Edward Elgar Publishing.

Costamagna, F. (2019) The European Social Union as a "union of national welfare states". Towards a European Social Union, *EU Visions*, 5 January 2019, http://www.euvisions.eu/the-european-social-union-as-a-union-of-national-welfare-states-a-legal-perspective/ (Accessed 3 March 2023).

Cunha, F., Heckman, J. (2007) The technology of skill formation. *The American Economic* Review, 97(2), pp. 31–47.

Darvas, Z., Anderson, J. (2020) *New Life for an Old Framework: Redesigning the European Union's Expenditure and Golden Fiscal Rules (CEWP 05/2020)*. Budapest: Corvinus University of Budapest.

Del Boca, D., Locatelli, M., Vuri, D. (2005) Child-care choices by working mothers: The case of Italy. *Review of Economics of the Household*, 3(4), pp. 453–477.

Dullien, S. (2014) *A European Unemployment Insurance Scheme: How to Provide for More Stability in the Eurozone*. Gütersloh: Verlag Bertelsmann Stiftung.

Esping-Andersen, G. (1996) Welfare states without work: The impasse of labour shedding and familialism in continental European social policy. In: Esping-Andersen, G. (eds) *Welfare States in Transition. National Adaptations in Global Economies.* London: Sage, pp. 66–87.

Ferrera, M. (2016) Impatient politics and social investment: The EU as 'policy facilitator. *Journal of European Public Policy*, 24(8), pp. 1–19.

Garben, S. (2019) The European pillar of social rights: An assessment of its meaning and significance. *Cambridge Yearbook of European Legal Studies*, 21, pp. 101–127.

Heckman, J.J. (2006) Skill formation and the economics of investing in disadvantaged children. *Science*, 312(5782), pp. 1900–1902.

Heidenreich, M. (eds) (2016) *Exploring Inequality in Europe: Diverging Income and Employment Opportunities in the Crisis.* Cheltenham: Edward Elgar Publishing.

Hemerijck, A. (2013) *Changing Welfare States.* Oxford: Oxford University Press.

Hemerijck, A. (2017) *The Uses of Social Investment.* Oxford: Oxford University Press.

Hemerijck, A. (2018) Social investment as a policy paradigm. *Journal of European Public Policy*, 25(6), pp. 810–827.

Hemerijck, A., Burgoon, B., Di Pietro, A. et al. (2016) *Assessing Social Investment Synergies (ASIS).* Brussels: Report written for the European Commission – DG-EMPL.

Hemerijck, A., Matsaganis, M. (forthcoming) *Who's Afraid of the Welfare State.* Oxford: Oxford University Press.

Hemerijck, A., Ronchi, S. (2020) Aprire la strada all'investimento sociale in un'Eurozona fragile. In: Ciarini, A. (ed) *Politiche di welfare e investimenti sociali.* Bologna: il Mulino, pp. 117–138.

Hemerijck, A., Ronchi, S. (2021) Recent developments: Social investment reform in the twenty-first century. In: Béland, D., Morgan, K.J., Herbert Obinger, H., Pierson, C. (eds.) *The Oxford Handbook of Welfare States (Second Edition).* Oxford: Oxford University Press, pp. 112–132.

Korpi, W., Ferrarini, T., Englund, S. (2013) Women's opportunities under different family policy constellations: Gender, class, and inequality tradeoffs in western countries re-examined. *Social Politics: International Studies in Gender, State & Society*, 20(1), pp. 1–40.

Kuitto, K., Helmdag, J. (2021) Extending working lives: How policies shape retirement and labour market participation of older workers. *Social Policy & Administration*, 55(3), pp. 423–439.

Kvist, J. (2013) The post-crisis European social model: Developing or dismantling social investments? *Journal of International and Comparative Social Policy*, 29(1), pp. 91–107.

Ladi, S., Tsarouhas, D. (2020) EU economic governance and Covid-19: Policy learning and windows of opportunity. *Journal of European Integration*, 42(8), pp. 1041–1056.

Lehwess-Litzmann, R., Nicaise, I. (2020) Surprisingly small: Effects of "generous" social benefits on re-employment of (quasi-) jobless households. *Journal of International and Comparative Social Policy*, 36(1), pp. 76–91.

Miró, J. (2021) Austerity's failures and policy learning: Mapping European Commission officials' beliefs on fiscal governance in the post-crisis EU. *Review of International Political Economy*, 28(5), pp. 1224–1248.

Moreira, A., Léon, M., Coda Moscarola, F., Roumpakis, A. (2021) In the eye of the storm . . . again! Social policy responses to COVID-19 in Southern Europe. *Social Policy & Administration*, 55, pp. 339–357.

Myles. J. (2002) A new social contract for the elderly? In: Esping-Andersen, G., Hemerijck, A., Gallie, D., Myles, J. (eds) *Why We Need a New Welfare State*. Oxford: Oxford University Press, pp. 130–172.

Natili, M., Negri, F., Ronchi, S. (2022) Widening double dualisation? Labour market inequalities and national social policy responses in Western Europe during the first wave of the COVID-19 pandemic *Social Policy & Administration*. https://doi.org/10.1111/spol.12814.

Nelson, M., Stephens, J.D. (2012) Do social investment policies produce more and better jobs? In: Morel, N., Palier, B., Palme, J. (eds) *Towards a Social Investment Welfare State?* Bristol: Policy Press, pp. 205–234.

Nieuwenhuis, R., Need, A., Van Der Kolk, H. (2012) Institutional and demographic explanations of women's employment in 18 OECD countries, 1975–1999. *Journal of Marriage and Family*, 74(3), pp. 614–630.

OECD. (1994) *The OECD Jobs Study: Facts, Analysis, Strategies*. Paris: OECD Publishing.

Okun, A.M. (1975) *Equality and Efficiency, the Big Tradeoff*. Washington, DC: Brookings Institution.

Ólafsson, S., Daly, M., Kangas, O., Palme, J. (eds) (2019) *Welfare and the Great Recession: A Comparative Study*. Oxford: Oxford University Press.

Petmesidou, M., Guillén, A.M. (2014) Can the welfare state as we know it survive? A view from the crisis-ridden South European Periphery. *South European Society and Politics*, 19(3), pp. 295–307.

Pierson, P. (2001) *The New Politics of the Welfare State*. Oxford: Oxford University Press.

Plavgo, I., Hemerijck, A. (2021) The social investment litmus test: Family formation, employment and poverty. *Journal of European Social Policy*, 31(3), pp. 282–296.

Ronchi, S. (2018) Which roads (if any) to social investment? The recalibration of EU welfare states at the crisis crossroads (2000–2014). *Journal of Social Policy*, 47(3), pp. 459–478.

Ronchi, S. (2019) *Boosting Work through Welfare? Individual-level Employment Outcomes of Social Investment across European Welfare States in the Crisis (EUI MWP Working Paper Red Number Series, 2019/44)*. Fiesole: European University Institute.

Rovny, A.E. (2014) The capacity of social policies to combat poverty among new social risk groups. *Journal of European Social Policy*, 24(5), pp. 405–423.

Streeck, W., Mertens, D. (2011) *Fiscal Austerity and Public Investment: Is the Possible the Enemy of the Necessary?* MPIfG Discussion Paper 11/12, Cologne, July 2011.

Taylor-Gooby, P. (eds) (2004) *New Risks, New Welfare: The Transformation of the European Welfare State*. Oxford and New York: Oxford University Press.

Vandenbroucke, F., Diri, S.R., Verbist, G. (2013) Excessive social imbalances and the performance of welfare states in the EU. *Euroforum Policy Paper*, 3, pp. 1–73.

Vandenbroucke, F. (2017) *Structural Convergence Versus Systems Competition: Limits to the Diversity of Labour Market Policies in the European Economic and Monetary Union* (ECFIN Discussion Paper 065). Brussels: European Commission Directorate-General for Economic and Financial Affairs.

Vandenbroucke, F., Hemerijck, A., Palier, B. (2011) *The EU Needs a Social Investment Pact*. Observatoire Social Européen Opinion Paper No. 5, May 2011.

Vandenbroucke, F., Barnard, C., De Baere, G. (eds) (2017) *A European Social Union after the Crisis*. Cambridge: Cambridge University Press.

Vandenbroucke, F., Andor, L., Beetsma, R.M., Burgoon, B., Fischer, G., Kuhn, T., Luigjes, C., Nicoli, F. (2020) *The European Commission's SURE Initiative and Euro Area Unemployment Re-insurance*. Brussels: VoxEU.

Vesan, P., Corti, F., Sabato, S. (2021) The European Commission's entrepreneurship and the social dimension of the European Semester: From the European pillar of social rights to the Covid-19 pandemic. *Comparative European Politics*, 19(3), pp. 277–295.

6   Minimum income and working time in the pluri-active society

Andrea Ciarini and Massimo Paci

6.1 A new phase in the development of the European welfare model?

The debate on new emerging social needs and on new active welfare policies represents a turning point in the long history of the European welfare state. This new phase, which has been defined as the 'recalibration' of the European welfare model (Ferrera et al. 2000), has, however, been marked, more or less evidently in recent years, by a 'neo-liberal' imprint, in line with the dominant economic creed in many European countries (Ferrera 2016; Ascoli et al. 2016). Many of the active policies launched in this phase, while distinguishing themselves from the previous 'passive' or 'compensatory' policies, introduce a contradictory element: the reintegration of the worker into the labour market, which often leads to unsatisfactory forms of employment in terms of their security and remuneration. It gives rise to precarious low-status jobs (e.g. the so-called 'mini-jobs' in Germany) and new forms of poverty, in addition to pre-existing forms of poverty. Basically, the new phase of welfare 'recalibration', which we have entered with activation policies, has shifted social protection from the simple level of compensation to the active reintegration of the worker. However, it does not seem to have eliminated the problem of job insecurity and poverty. This is partly because in the field of public policy, in many countries reforms have tended to introduce several types of subsidies aimed at supplementing low incomes, whilst not doing much to counteract the poverty risk associated with work (ibid; Grady 2017). As a direct result, the increase in employment thus generated has often not led automatically to a reduction in poverty (Saraceno 2016).

The spread of the in-work poverty does not only depend on social policies. The negative changes in the structure of inequalities have also been important (Piketty 2016; Stiglitz 2019), as well as the impact of the new dualisms that have formed in the labour market and in access to welfare protections. This has been shown in comparative political

DOI: 10.4324/9781003369707-6

economy studies (Palier and Thelen 2010) as well as within the critical literature on social investment (Cantillon 2011; Cantillon and Van Lancker 2013; Bonoli). These problems are then combined with the issue of polarisation, a phenomenon about which there has recently been a growing debate within the field of labour market studies. From different perspectives (Goos and Manning 2007; Autor 2015; Bachmann et al. 2019), the progressive decline of medium-skilled occupations and the simultaneous growth of the lower and upper parts of the labour market are commonly referred to as polarisation. The resulting disorienting effect contributes to an even more articulated dualisations within the labour market. Alongside the dualism between the high-skilled and the low-skilled, which can be traced back to the transition to the knowledge economy (Palier and Thelen 2010), polarisation adds the problem of the downward slide of the medium-skilled, who have been partially protected from it so far, with the more immediate effect of increasingly strong competition for the same low-skilled jobs (Marchal and Marx 2018). Consequently, there is even more of a downward spiral in the spread of poor jobs. There are several underlying factors behind this phenomenon. The first, and for many the main one, concerns automation in the workplace by applied technologies, with a displacement effect that increasingly pushes down groups of medium-skilled workers. The second relates to delocalisation processes, that is, the gradual shift of mainly medium- and low-skilled manufacturing and industrial jobs to newly industrialised countries. That too contributes to the narrowing of the middle section of the labour market, resulting in increased competition in the lower tertiary sector for the same jobs.

Although in different forms and to different extents in different countries, all these transformations contribute to increasing the extent of the working poor, with new demands for social protection to which policies are called upon to respond. We have seen in Chapter 3 that social policies, especially minimum income policies, risk feeding this circuit of in-work poverty, modifying and worsening the overall quality of the work that is created or supported, directly or indirectly. Faced with the alternative of budgetary cuts, policy makers reforming minimum income schemes have often opted for increasing the means tests and selection criteria for beneficiaries, thus setting up a system based on subsidies legitimising and reproducing poor work. The latter is found in productive and even reproductive spheres, for example, through subsidies being conditional on community service work. The question we ask ourselves at this point is: is it possible to trace a possible alternative to this option? And to what extent can the structural transformations affecting work (outsourcing, polarisation, and digitalisation of the economy) be rebalanced by a different way of conceiving income support? Here we come to the heart of the problems addressed in this chapter.

The analysis we intend to develop aims at identifying interventions capable of making minimum income compatible with the enhancement of non-market activities: care, civic and voluntary commitment, and training. All this, however, is not intended as a condition for accessing some kind of social benefit, a subsidy, or a minimum income, but as a universal right of the citizen linked to a different 'chosen', rather than suffered, work-life balance. For a number of reasons, the time has come for a reassessment of this ratio of work to life, which necessarily includes the issue of working time.

The chapter is organised as follows: in Section 6.2, we will give an overview of the theoretical coordinates of the debate on polarisation and its effects on the labour market. Section 6.3 relates these transformations to the challenges that welfare policies are facing. Starting from this, in the Sections 6.4, 6.5, and 6.6, we will focus on minimum income policies in their different articulations with reference to those strands of literature that have focused on the issue of market and non-market activation. The fifth and last paragraph recalls some conclusive considerations on the issues of work-life balance in the framework of a reform agenda inspired by the SI objectives.

6.2 Polarisation, technological innovation and labour transformations

Despite being a medium- to long-term phenomenon (Bachmann et al. 2019), research on the phenomenon of polarisation has steadily increased in recent years. The growing number of studies that have been conducted at the international level (Goos and Manning 2007; Autor 2015; Bachmann et al. 2019) is proof of this; these studies have largely focused on the consequences of technological transition in the workplace. As has been pointed out by several authors (Autor 2015; Eichhorst et al. 2016) technological change does not impact generically upon work, but tends to differentiate according to the degree of replication and standardisation of different work tasks, regardless of their intellectual or manual nature. This aspect is very important in terms of polarisation, because it is the basis for the increase both in more skilled jobs and in less skilled jobs, which can only be performed by workers. On the other hand, as a result of these transformations, average professionalism in sales, administration, or production is decreasing. It is more routine and replicable and for this reason, Autor (2015) argues, it is more easily replaced by automation or the spread of algorithms. The resulting employment framework tends to narrow amongst the medium-skilled and to increase amongst the high- and low-skilled. That the employment picture tends to shrink in these components is also confirmed by other estimates, such as those provided by the OECD (2016;

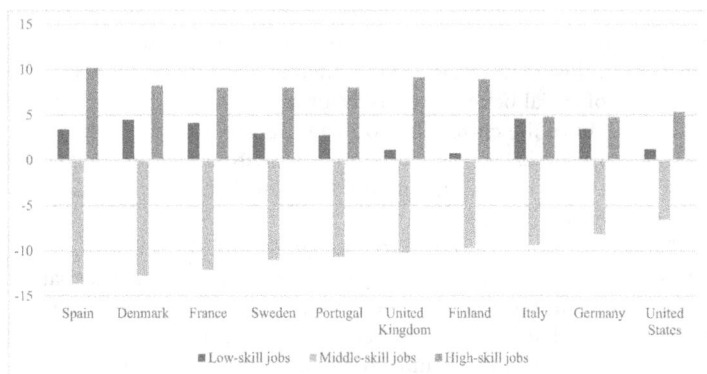

Figure 6.1 Employment rate change in Europe (EU28 average) and the United
States by occupational skill level, Val. %, Years 2002–2014

Source: Our elaboration on OECD data

see Figure 6.1), according to which the most significant employment
losses between 2002 and 2014 occurred in the more routine medium-
skilled jobs in Europe and the USA. On the other hand, it is pointed out
that both high-skilled and low-skilled jobs increased, many of them in
the low-productivity tertiary sectors: trade, food services, but also care,
which represent today one of the major sources of new employment,
although often at risk of poverty because of the very low wage levels.

That said, if the focus shifts from flows and stocks to the content
and organisation of work, further issues emerge that require further
investigation. This aspect is all the more important if one takes into account the differences that tend, for example, to differentiate industry
and manufacturing sectors, on the one hand, and services on the other,
which are in turn distinguishable in sub-sectors that are differentiated
in terms of work content, skills, and the use of technologies applied
to work.

As Guarascio and Sacchi (2017) correctly remarked, the reference to
automation applied to production – especially industrial production –
is not indicative of a generalised trend, likely to be replicated with the
same characteristics in other sectors. In services, for example, the drive
to multiply supply (brought about by technologies) does not necessarily
go hand in hand with skill improvement and the quality of work, as can
be expected in some industries. Just think about the tensions and problems faced by platform workers in this case, regarding which several
authors (Huws 2014; Degryse 2016; Pulignano 2019) have highlighted
how the almost total lack of regulation in the area of contractual rights

(pay, welfare, and working conditions) facilitated by the web exposes these workers both to low wages and stressful work schedules between the (unpaid) time they have to devote to the job or order search on the platform and the request to perform the service quickly (through technology) to obtain a remuneration aligned with that of a regular employment agreement.

The drift towards deregulation and disintermediation arising from these contexts increases the downward pressure on labour, with negative consequences in terms of growing inequality, income inequality, and job security. These issues are, to all intents and purposes, different from those found in the industrial sector, where digitisation can also lead to an enrichment of work content and an improvement in skill levels, albeit for an increasingly smaller number of workers.

In such a fragmented scenario of conflicting dynamics, what we know most for sure is that, for the moment, two trends tend to emerge, upgrading and polarisation, which are different but not necessarily opposed to each other. Under the impetus of technological change, labour markets are indeed undergoing a qualitative change that favours the creation of high-skilled, high-value-added jobs at the top levels, even if it is conceivable that this process has affected only a few occupations. At the same time, the simultaneous reduction in medium-skilled jobs contributes to increasing the amount of low-skilled and low-paid work, which is already growing in the low-productivity service sectors.

Both the upgrading and polarisation theses agree on one point, namely that the changes underway will mainly affect the reduction of middle jobs, middle skills and, ultimately, the middle classes. On this point, both theories seem to converge, although from different starting points. In the case of the upgrading, we are faced with a process of improving skills and competencies that leads some, if only a few, to improve their chances of upward mobility in the labour market. Polarisation, in contrast, involves the downward slide of large parts of the traditional middle classes. The consequences of all this for social protection systems are likely to be severe. It is in fact around the central role of the 'middle classes' that the welfare systems have historically been built. And this, as Palier (2019) points out, both in terms of the beneficiaries of the measures and, no less importantly, their financing, whether it be tax- or contribution-based.

6.3 Welfare challenges in the face of technological transition

These problems pose significant challenges for European welfare systems. If, on the one hand, a 'productive' welfare agenda is crucial for a high level of competition (as it is the goal of the SI), on the other hand, it does not avoid the problem of poor and precarious jobs that tends to affect also mid-siders, pushed to the margins of the labour market as a consequence of polarisation. Are active labour market policies enough for these workers? It is clear that in the face of such a problem, the presence of a structured income support network. Hemerijck (2017) has also recently stressed this point in his redefinition of the institutional basis of the SI, seen as a combination of three fundamental functions: Stock (education and human capital), Flow (activation, labour insertion, and work-life balance), and Buffer (social safety nets and minimum income policies). Together with the relaunch of expenditure on education, research, and care services for active participation in the labour market, Hemerijck (ibid) adds the importance of buffers, that is, income protection measures aimed at coping with the different phases of life cycle transition. Compared to the first theoretical approaches to SI, there is in this new articulation of interventions the recognition of the necessary integration between actions to support the transition to higher added value production and income protection measures in the form of a guaranteed minimum income (see also Hemerijck and Ronchi in this volume).

But even in relation to the problem of polarisation, this idea of integration has begun to make headway. In order to temper its negative effects, some scholars (Oesch 2013) have suggested the adoption of integrated passive and active measures. On the one hand by investing public resources in tertiary education, so as to allow firms to access a highly qualified workforce able to take full advantage of technological progress, and on the other hand by strengthening upper secondary education and vocational training for low-skilled and low-wage workers, supporting these wages through the establishment of a minimum income (Oesch 2013, pp. 8–9). In this same line of intervention, the guaranteed minimum income, as a dedicated anti-poverty measure, also plays a buffer function, supporting incomes for those who are exposed to the poverty trap. It is no coincidence that in many countries combinations of this kind, between minimum income and minimum wage, tend to be on the list of the responses to combat the phenomenon of in-work poverty and precarious work. Even the OECD (2019), in its report on the future of work, acknowledged the need to strengthen income protection measures disconnected from the contributory mechanism, in order to cope with the growing conditions of insecurity and precariousness that prevail in short-term contracts, especially in the grey areas between dependence and independence that are increasingly encountered in different sectors impacted by technologies, starting with platforms. All this has obvious policy implications. Whether it relates to the impact of technology on the social groups most at risk of substitution or to the issue of labour in the transition to the 'service economy', there is a call to strengthen income protection mechanisms, starting with minimum income policies. Indeed, these policies came with many expectations, not only the (original) one of coping with situations of extreme poverty but also income support for the working poor (Natili 2018).

6.4 Participation income and the pluri-active society

The debate on the review of minimum income policies raises issues of different magnitude. Some concern the institutional design among services, direct transfers, tax credits, active labour policies, and economic supports for housing, health, and childcare (Marchal and Marx 2018). Others reflect more general theoretical issues. At this level, minimum income brings with it an internal duplicity which has been present since it appeared on the scene many years ago. On the one hand, minimum income can be considered as a conditional anti-poverty measure targeting certain population groups at higher risk of poverty. On the other hand, the minimum income can be considered a universal measure, covering all citizenship without any work conditionality and obligations. Moreover, it is not accompanied, as in the case of minimum guaranteed incomes, by ancillary benefits in the form of contributions to housing payments, food or other consumer goods (Van Parijs and Vanderborght 2019), but provides an individual basis that in the intentions of the proponents contributes to freeing people from the 'unemployment trap' and precariousness.

(ibid)

In its first conception, the minimum income does not present any substantial new aspects, being part of the traditional measures of economic assistance and labour inclusion for the poor, including the working poor. In its second meaning, on the other hand, we are faced with a real 'phase change' in the history of welfare: it will no longer be only workers or the poor who would be the beneficiaries of the new social protection measure, but all citizens, rich and poor, as long as they belong to a specific national community. In Van Parijs's proposal (1995; see also Standing 2014), the 'basic income', which is not linked to work and the contributory mechanisms for financing social benefits, is considered a form of emancipating social intervention, that is, designed to encourage mobility between one job and another and to free up time to devote to other activities outside the market: education, care activities, and voluntary work.

Already in the 1980s, in the theoretical framework of some authors, such as Ralf Dahrendorf (1988), the idea of a new 'society of activities' emerged, in which market work even assumed a secondary role. Subsequently, it resonated particularly with the contribution of Alain Supiot (2003), who, summarising the idea of the legal and economic recognition of non-market activities, proposed the granting of specific 'social drawing rights' (droits de tirage sociaux).

> in which the time spent to perform them can be assimilated to working time according to labour and social security law, such as the activity of caring for people, the activity of training and job search and voluntary activities of collective interest.
>
> (ibid. p. 90)

The discussion concerning these non-market activities, on the other hand, has often gone hand in hand with discussion of the reduction of working hours, through the development of leave and especially the spread of part-time work.

Among the authors who have combined the idea of non-market activities with that of working time, it is worth mentioning Tony Atkinson (1996, 2015), with his proposal for a 'participation income' as a basic level of universal transfer to be juxtaposed to a market labour income. It is to be kept low in order not to favour displacement effects on labour supply. Atkinson's proposal does not exclude forms of conditionality for the provision of participation income. However, they are not linked to activation in the labour market, but to non-market activities such as voluntary work, care and assistance, continuous training, and further education.

The concept of a 'pluri-active' society (Paci 2005) is based on a similar interpretation but within a broader consideration of the changes in work in all its forms. This is intended to emphasise the need for welfare reforms aimed at including within their scope, with appropriate forms of legal and monetary recognition, the many fields of activity outside the market: care, assistance, and voluntary commitment, which already occupy an important space in welfare systems. This interpretation does not deny the value and importance of paid work, even in welfare. But it starts with the recognition that not all social services can and should be provided through public or market services.

Paci's interpretation (2005, in particular: 184 et seq.) propels us towards a pluri-active society characterised by a high level of innovation and productivity, in which, alongside market work, a series of socially recognised non-market activities carried out by citizens are valued, such as, for example, study, apprenticeship, and training; care work and assistance to children and the elderly; voluntary work; and artistic and cultural work. In this interpretation, non-market activities are not to be understood as one of the conditionalities to access an unemployment benefit or minimum income. In Italy, (free) community work is one of the requirements to access the minimum guaranteed income. Differently, in the pluri-active society conception, it is a right guaranteed to all citizens on the basis of their wishes, including the right to reduce working hours (for the same wage) to free up time to devote to other spheres of activity. The modalities of this recognition are of a different kind (Paci 2005 pp. 156–167). Some forms of this recognition are already present, varying widely. On the one hand, there has been an expansion of forms of 'suspension' of work without salary reduction (leave; sabbaticals, etc.). On the other hand, there has been an expansion of the allowances or subsidies paid to those who carry out such non-market activities (such as support for family caregiving, including notional contributions for caregivers). This process of legal and economic recognition does not only concern caregiving, study, and training activities, but also those of civic and voluntary commitment, as is the case, for example, in Italy for the universal civic service: a form of monetary recognition (EUR 444 per months) for young people who choose to be involved in care activities, international cooperation, the protection of cultural heritage or activities linked to social and environmental sustainability for a period of 8 to 12 months. These activities, while remaining outside the labour market, nevertheless acquire their own autonomy and a 'para-labour' identity. In France, a scheme has recently been introduced, 'the compte d'engagement citoyen', that legally recognises the engagement of citizens in activities outside the labour market. Thus, they are able to benefit from an annual amount of freely chosen vocational training, costing up to EUR 720 per year. Together with two other schemes: the 'compte personel de formation' and the 'compte professionel de prevention', it is part of a set of measures that are based on a citizen's subjective rights (see also Ferrera 2019). They ensure access to accredited training initiatives, and lastly use time as a new criteria to define the content of welfare protection, allowing beneficiaries to better combine work obligations and off-market activities.

6.5 New needs and new work: towards new welfare policies?

The debate on pluri-activity is closely linked to the transformations we have just outlined. Polarisation, poor work, and the impact of technology may have consequences for the quantity and quality of available work. And some of those are already evident, as we have just seen. In particular, the main problem currently is the reduction in the number of medium-skilled occupations, resulting in increased downward competition for the same jobs. However, technology does imply not only the displacement of some market jobs but also a possible time-release, (increase in free time) due to the fact that more is produced with less labour and with productivity gains, or at least with reduced costs for companies. This aspect calls into question several issues, relating to the inequalities that are thus produced, for example, between those who suffer from polarisation and those who instead manage to take advantage of the upgrading to higher-skilled jobs. But it is equally important to raise the question of how to use this productivity or how to allocate it for social protection.

Faced with the problem of labour displacement, the various reform hypotheses can be grouped into three main options. The first aims at strengthening social safety nets and especially policies to combat poverty, so as to meet the demands for protection of the most vulnerable in the current transition. The second concerns the establishment of an unconditional basic income for all. The third aims instead at a controlled reduction of market working hours and consequently time-release into other, economically and legally recognised non-market activities. This perspective does not prefigure a differentiated strategy between the few winners and the losers of the technological transition which reflects the two movements of polarisation and upgrading mentioned earlier. If anything, it envisages a reorganisation of protection for all within a framework of controlled reduction of working time within the market. On the other hand, while it is true that throughout history technological revolutions have contributed to the creation of new job opportunities, it is also true that in the long run working hours have also steadily reduced. Today, it is inconceivable to think of working a 12-hour day, seven days a week. Yet, as Ralf Dahrendorf (1988) had already pointed out in the 1980s, this was the case for a long time (Castel 1995). Yet, even here, productivity increases, new technologies and, no less important, the pressures and claims of workers and trade-unions made it possible to reduce working hours, guaranteeing new social benefits. Without taking into account the French 35 hours (the main attempt to impose by legislation the reduction of working time) we are now in a favourable situation for this reflection to be intertwined with the prospect of a controlled reduction of working time at the same wage. Through collective bargaining, agreements to reduce working time have spread in several European countries. Consider, for example, the experimental agreement concluded in Germany in the Baden Wuerttemberg region involving 900,000 workers in the metalworking sector. It allows for a reduction in working hours, from 35 to 28 hours, for a minimum period of six months and a maximum of 24, in the event of family care needs. The agreement ensures that no more than 10% of the applications per individual company can be accepted and that there is an increase in flexi-time up to a maximum of 40 hours per week on a voluntary basis to compensate the company. More recently, in the United Kingdom on of the biggest trial of a four-day working week has been launched, involving more than 3000 staff members and 70 firms, mostly tech companies. The pandemic had a profound impact on labour markets, accelerating trends towards reduced working time. On the one hand, many countries adopted programmes to incentive agreements for working hour reductions. On the other hand, the spread of smart working contributes to reorganise working activities, renewing interest in issues related to the relationship between working time and productivity. However, they also present critical points. These trials are unlikely to cover economic sectors that are more marginal or where bargaining power is weak. From this point of view, they do not prevent the development of new dualisms, namely between those who have the chance to benefit from options of this type thanks to their professional status or type of company, and on the other hand, those who remain excluded not only from work in the market but also from non-market work economically recognised by a contract. It would be different if these options were included in a general reassessment of work-life balance for all.

In Italy, the standard working week is set at 40 hours, one of the longest in Europe. While unemployment is still high, any reduction in working hours is more often involuntary, for example, through the growth of involuntary part-time work. Figure 6.2 shows that the average number of hours worked – 36.5 between 2009 and 2018 is steady. However, this is still below pre-crisis levels (Istat 2019) and involuntary part-time work has increased for all age groups, highlighting a problem

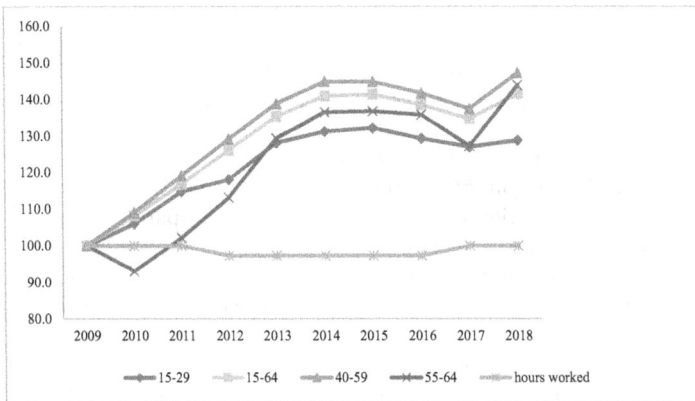

Figure 6.2 Involuntary part-time and working hours in Italy, 2009 = 100, Years 2009–2018

Source: Our elaboration on Eurostat and Istat data

that particularly affects Italian women. Approximately two-thirds of the increase in involuntary part-time work involves women and accounts for 19.5% of female employment (ibid), which is increasing but of low quality.

The paradox is that while there is a high level of involuntary part-time work and people working for only a few hours, there are others who work well over 40 hours a week, and they are benefitted by the overtime tax relief measures introduced by governments in recent years. On the other hand, with regards to informal caregiving, the data tell us that family care work has also increased during the same period, especially for women. In the first place is the fact that Italy is the European country with the highest gender gap in the distribution of paid market-work and unpaid non-market work. In other words, while men work much more in the labour market, women are much more present in the family. They work about 3 hours more per day than men, and home working amounts to 75% of their working day. This means that more than half of women are burdened with paid work, and with unpaid work, and 54.7% work 60 hours a week. Among men, fewer than half, 47.3%, work these hours. That said, time dedicated to family care is also increasing. For many men, this increase is accompanied by a reduction in paid work. This is particularly true for those who have suffered most from the crisis, for example by reducing their working hours in order to retain their jobs (Istat 2019).

The negative consequences of economic stagnation are hidden behind these data, from the return to pre-crisis employment levels, with more people employed, but working far fewer hours, to the role of involuntary part-time employment as an alternative to unemployment. In more general terms, we can say that the scenario of the pluri-active society is now a fact, but more as an obligatory alternative, especially for women, rather than as the outcome of a free choice.

Apart from a purely economic approach, the right to balance market and non-market labour is about enlarging the sphere of universal citizens' rights. Secondly, it is not antithetical to the development of social investment-oriented policies. They are two separate but mutually related spheres. The objectives set by social investment are of paramount importance for improving human capital, and supporting an ever better-qualified labour force and sectors with higher productivity. Training and active labour policies play a strategic role to respond to the pressures of digitisation. Inside and outside the labour market, Stock and Flow can help to ensure that skills are constantly improved, all the more so given the problem of the present nature of professional skills, which become rapidly outdated. At the same time, it is equally important to invest in welfare services in order to ensure that they match emerging social needs, be they related to care, work-life balance, or lifecycle labour market transitions. These investments also have the potential to generate new jobs, both directly and indirectly.

Employment in welfare services is also less impacted by the displacement effects, as Palier recently wrote in reference to the impacts of digitisation on welfare systems (2019). For many of these services, the problems concern, if anything, the downward pressure on labour costs, which we have dealt with in the previous chapters, and the fact that the services are not accessible to all, especially in some countries.

But, if the welfare state is disrupted, providing a basic income to all will not enable everyone to purchase these services on the market. Rather, it is by investing in collective and social goods, services and social infrastructures that these downward adjustments can be counteracted. That said, a long-term investment policy in the strategic areas of social investment does not exclude investing also in individual pluriactivity, that is, in balancing the different spheres of activity, formal and informal, in parallel with a reduction in working hours in market employment.

Several studies have confirmed a positive relationship between reduced working hours and productivity. Conversely, they point out that long working hours, as well as leading to increased stress and risks to physical health, in the long run, lead to lower productivity. Now, if we look at these aspects from a broader perspective, that is, also in the light of technology-induced transformation, we can envisage viable solutions. The point is to redirect innovation and productivity generated by the technological transition in the direction of people's desires and not only those who introduce these innovations, that is, companies and their shareholders. While digitisation reduces the workforce, at least in some sectors, productivity gains and cost reductions for companies can provide a fiscal basis for financing new welfare schemes aimed at economically and legally recognising the 'social' activation of non-market activity, as a universal right guaranteed to all citizens. The alternative is not to regulate these processes, leaving it to technology to rearrange living and working time. As in other transitional phases, rethinking the general structures of production and reproduction is a challenge. Besides, if technological development and automation will make it possible to produce more with relatively lower employment, and if there is continuous training to update skills for the new production contexts, the issue of the fair distribution of the benefits deriving from digitisation must also be addressed. Work less, work all, has been a slogan in the past used to redistribute labour. We cannot exclude that in the future 'working less' may be associated with a commitment to non-market activity areas being recognised, not with a salary but with appropriate economic and legal protections aimed at enhancing the pluri-activity of individuals.

References

Ascoli, U., Ranci, C., Sgritta, G.B., (eds) (2016) *Investire nel sociale. La difficile innovazione del welfare italiano*. Bologna: il Mulino.

Atkinson, A.B. (1996) The case for a participation income. *The Political Quarterly*, 67(1), pp. 67–70.

Atkinson, T. (2015) *Inequalities. What Can Be Done*. Oxford: Oxford University Press.

Autor, D. (2015) Why are there still so many jobs? The history and future of workplace automation. *The Journal of Economic Perspectives*, 3, pp. 3–30.

Bachmann, R., Cim, M., Green, C. (2019) Long-run patterns of labour market polarization: Evidence from German micro data. *British Journal of Industrial Relations*, 57(2), pp. 350–376.

Cantillon, B. (2011) The paradox of the social investment state: Growth, employment and poverty in the Lisbon era. *Journal of European Social Policy*, 21(5), pp. 432–449.

Cantillon, B., Van Lancker, W. (2013) Three shortcomings of the social investment perspective. *Social Policy and Society*, 12(4), pp. 553–564.

Castel, R. (1995) *Les Métamorphose de la question sociale. Unechronique du salariat*. Paris: Fayard.

Dahrendorf, R. (1988) *Per un nuovo liberalismo*. Roma-Bari: Laterza.

Degryse, C. (2016) *Digitalisation of the Economy and Its Impact on Labour Markets* (Working Paper 2016.02). Brussels: ETUI. www.etui.org/Publications2/Working-Papers/ Digitalisation-of-the-economy-and-its-impact-on-labour-markets

Eichhorst, W., Hinte, H., Rinne, U., Tobsch V. (2016) *How Big is the Gig? Assessing the Preliminary Evidence on the Effects of Digitalization on the Labor Market*. IZA Policy Paper, n. 117, Bonn, October 2016.

Ferrera, M. (2016) *Rotta di collisione. Euro contro welfare?* Roma-Bari: Laterza.

Ferrera, M. (2019) *La società del Quinto Stato*. Roma-Bari: Laterza.

Ferrera, M., Hemerijck, A., Rhodes, M. (2000) *The Future of Social Europe: Recasting Work and Welfare in the New Economy* (Report prepared for the Portuguese Presidency of the EU). Oeiras: Celta Editora.

Goos, M., Manning, A. (2007) Lousy and lovely jobs: The rising polarization of work in Britain. *The Review of Economics and Statistics*, 89(1), pp. 118–33.

Grady, J. (2017) The state, employment, and regulation: Making work not pay. *Employee Relations*, 39(3), pp. 274–290.

Guarascio, D., Sacchi, S. (2017) *Digitalizzazione, automazione e futuro del lavoro*. Paper, INAPP, November 2017.

Hemerijck, A. (eds) (2017) *The Uses of Social Investment*. Oxford: Oxford University Press.

Huws, U. (2014) *Labor in the Global Digital Economy: The Cybertariat Comes of Age*. New York: NYU Press.

ISTAT (2019) *I tempi della vita quotidiana – Lavoro, conciliazione, parità di genere e benessere soggettivo*. Roma: Rapporto.

Marchal, S., Marx, I. (2018) Stemming the tide: What have EU countries done to support low-wage workers in an era of downward wage pressures? *Journal of European Social Policy*, 28(1), pp. 18–33.

Natili, M. (2018) The politics of minimum income. In: *Explaining Path Departure and Policy Reversal in the Age of Austerity*. London: Palgrave Macmillan.

OECD. (2016) *Automation and Independent Work in a Digital Economy* (Policy brief on the future of work). Paris: OECD.

OECD. (2019) *OECD Employment Outlook 2019. The Future of Work.* Paris: OECD.

Oesch, D. (2013) *Occupational Change in Europe: How Technology and Education Transform the Job Structure.* Oxford: Oxford University Press.

Paci, M. (2005) *Nuovi Lavori, Nuovo Welfare.* Bologna: Il Mulino.

Palier, B. (2019) Work, social protection and the middle classes: What future in the digital age? *International Social Security Review,* 72(3), pp. 113–133.

Palier, B., Thelen, K. (2010) Institutionalizing dualism: Complementarities and change in France and Germany. *Politics & Society,* 1, pp. 119–148.

Piketty, T. (2016) *Il capitale nel XXI secolo.* Milano: Bompiani.

Pulignano, V. (2019) *Work in Deregulated Labour Markets: A Research Agenda for Precariousness.* European Trade Union Institute, Working Paper, n. 3, Brussels, April 2019.

Saraceno, C. (2016) *Il lavoro non basta. La povertà in Europa negli anni della crisi.* Milano: Feltrinelli.

Standing, G. (2014) *A Precariat Charter: From Denizens to Citizens.* London: Bloomsbury Academic.

Stiglitz, J.E. (2019) *People, Power, and Profits: Progressive Capitalism for an Age of Discontent.* New York: W. W. Norton & Company.

Supiot, A. (2003) *Il futuro del lavoro. Trasformazioni dell'occupazione e prospettive della regolazione del lavoro.* Roma: Carocci.

Van Parijs, P. (1995) *Real Freedom for All.* Oxford: Oxford University Press.

Van Parijs, P., Vanderborght, Y. (2019) *Basic Income: A Radical Proposal for a Free Society and a Sane Economy.* Cambridge, MA: Harvard: Harvard University.

Index

For Product Safety Concerns and Information please contact our EU
representative GPSR@taylorandfrancis.com
Taylor & Francis Verlag GmbH, Kaufingerstraße 24, 80331 München, Germany

9 781032 439778